Praise for *The Astonishing JOY Novella*

"I do not give lectures or a little charity. When I give, I give myself."
—Walt Whitman

Whitman's quote describes Dianne exactly. She gifts her dear friends endlessly. And whatever the gift, you know it was from her heart. Her book takes us on her personal journey as a gift she wholeheartedly wants to share with everyone. She reveals the courage, love, laughter, creativity, and fears that it took to arrive at JOY!!.

Di, as she is known to friends, has been a good friend since the late 60's. You get to know someone intimately when you live together as we did when we were roommates for the year our husbands were called to active duty in Viet Nam. Being a person that always explores new ways to meet a challenge, she was determined the year was not going to be one of loneliness and fear. Every week, we rearranged our living space. Painting classes, exercise classes, and exploring new recipes made the time fly. It is no surprise that she shares some of her story through her cooking experiences. Coming from recipes of a small rural Kansas farming community to complicated recipes she enjoyed fixing for multiple guests, the kitchen never defeated her.

Nor is she defeated as a seeker. I know she will continue to grow in her Joy. Di and I had many parallel life experiences as the years progressed. In the 70's when we both were making career changes, she went the way of fine art, and I entered the criminal justice system. As I look back, we were both exploring our second chances and digging to find our purpose in life. Work that took years of setbacks and rewards but resulted in possibilities of giving others a way to a second chance. Di's book is a genuine offering to personal fulfillment.

Marilyn Scafe, Retired
Chair, Kansas Parole Board
Director, Kansas Reentry Policy Council

I found the Joy Novella to be a thoughtful, provocative, and delightful narrative. The Astonishing Joy Novella compels us to review where our true loyalty lies, where our core belief resides. And therefore, powerfully asks us to examine how we choose to live this precious gift of life. Dianne points out that the Scriptures have cautioned us not to walk with unbelievers. Beautifully written with inspiration from the Holy Spirit, Dianne's straightforward, heartfelt, inspirational nuggets of Truth as interpreted from the Lord's Prayer, are easy to understand and transform into a potent everyday practice. Dianne's application of this movement within a partnership can encourage a transition in relation ship that empowers a shift in the basic foundation of a marriage.

The breakdown of the steps to activate these principles in my own relationship, bring me to a point of recommitting to 'my first love,' as Dianne calls her dedication to the Lord. Dianne demonstrates to us, once you are Born Again, our every action reflects the deepest Truth that 'Now I am in Him, and He is in me.' Her examples lead us to also set aside lesser pursuits to fulfill in a very specific way, the greatest of the Commandments: to 'Love the Lord, My God, with my whole heart and mind and soul.' Dianne gifts us with her deeper understanding and the powerful declaration that as we lift one, we lift all. Matthew 25:40 'Truly, I say to you, as you did it to one of the least of these my brothers, you did it to me.'

Nancy Lapari

Enjoy the inspirational words on these pages from a beautiful daughter of the Most High God.

I've known Dianne my whole life. She has always been a mentor for me throughout many trials, and I have always respected her advice. Her life has been a testimony to the work of the Holy Spirit, but for several years now, she has carried the Holy Spirit fire for our Father. Having walked together on this narrow path with the Light of the Word, I can say with assurance that her study of the Holy Scriptures has become her greatest passion. Astonishing Joy Novella is filled with many hope-filled scriptural references attesting to Dianne's steadfast assurance in the Lord Who sustains her. Chapter One is the foundational chapter to understand the rest of the book. A believer's greatest desire is to know

God. Exodus 33:13 says, "If I have found favor in your eyes, please show me your ways so I may know You and continue to find favor with You". Dianne lays out many scriptures referencing what it means to make God the priority in your life.

I would highly recommend this book to anyone who wants to draw closer to the Father through the work of Yeshua, the only means to salvation and eternal life and the guidance of the Holy Spirit. Her work is touching, inspiring, engaging, and full of flavor for anyone who seeks a "recipe" for navigating through this world. "For the battle is not yours, but God's" 2 Chronicles 20:15 / "For the joy of the Lord is your strength!" Psalm 73:26 / "I will lift up my eyes to the mountains—from where does my help come? My help comes from the Lord, the Maker of Heaven and Earth" Psalm 121:1-2.

Barbara Reed, A Lover of Jesus

The author takes you on a great adventure – no, a journey through her life: flashbacks to her childhood, reflections on her growth in the knowledge of God, and her astute portrayal of God's word as she brings you to today and the future. You become her real friend as she invites you into the heart of her home, the kitchen, and into her heart as she lures you in for her love of God. For you see, her trials and tribulations are very similar to yours. With her stories and God's scripture, you begin to realize you are never alone. Her journey brings us to the realization we all encounter; that we must put God first. Her trials and tribulations and "ah-ha" moments are so vivid and real, you can't help but relate. She laces her "pearls of wisdom" with God's word to help guide us forward. This book even seasons everything with a dash of hope. It's a great read and her pearls of wisdom are great for us always. I am blessed to be able to make this journey with her and God. They have truly enriched my soul.

Cathy G.

Dianne Congdon's new book is a lovely, resonant path of spiritual discovery. Some passages remind one of scriptural precepts long known and practiced; others shine new light on familiar disciplines bringing a bright 'Aha!' flash of insight. I love the Chef Notes, the tender peeks into Dianne's personal past or the lives of others.

These colorful, quirky anecdotes, testimonies really, infuse her spiritual teaching with vibrancy, making her reader a part of the memory or illustration, sparking personal life application. The Joy Novella is discipleship for every maturity level of Believer from just saved to having served Jesus for a lifetime. Plunge in to be refreshed, renewed, and matured in your faith walk of joy!

Shelli L Miller, Executive Assistant and Communications Director, Empower 2000

This book will empower you every time you read it! It is full of God's anointing and scriptures that will motivate you to pray and seek God's face daily. It will cause you to know the goodness and strength of the Lord when you read it! I will advise anyone feeling at their lowest point to read this book to be encourage and enlightened.

Brenda Amstead

The Astonishing JOY Novella

Recipes for Renewal

Seven Petitions to Heal a Heavy Heart

Dianne Congdon

DEDICATION

To the person of the Holy Spirit
who fills me with Hope and Joy

To my Beloved Parents,
Frank and Agnes Jurenka

and

To my Beloved Husband,
Bob

and to our Children:
Abby, Bill, John, and Sheila.

A Tribute to My Parents
Frank and Agnes Breford Jurenka

I want to take this opportunity to honor and bless you for your character and virtuous deeds throughout your life. I honor you for the years of selfless service spent in raising my brother Frank and I, for providing for our material, emotional, and spiritual needs. I honor you for preferring our needs over your own and for the sacrifices you made for our sake.

My beautiful parents met at a barn dance. I recall my mother showing me this barn and exactly how it all happened. As I look back and reflect about those times of my growing up in Holyrood, I could cry. So precious and orderly was my life. What a blessing to live in trust. I was always protected, loved, and cherished in this small Czech farming community forged by early Kansas pioneers.

My parents were quiet and faithful to their simple life. If I walked out to the street and looked down several blocks, I would see wheat waving in the fields. My mother and father were married in 1930. Dad worked in the oilfields and Mom managed our home and all things from her kitchen! Imagine that we never locked our doors except one time when we went on vacation to see Mount Rushmore.

Dad and Mom took my brother and me to church every Sunday. Dad made his family a priority. We had dinner together every night. We had gardens, chickens, and chores. I remember when milk was delivered in glass jars. We had large family gatherings on both my mother and my father's side of the family. That's just what families did to stay unified and in support of each other.

I grew up listening to the radio. In 1956 we got our first TV. My brother, Frank, who is 5 years older was smart and clever. I could write another book about his antics with his buddies.

My parents were very humble and would help our neighbors. These values were observed not instructed. You see, the small town took care of its own. My brother and I knew Dad's rules were firm. I honor and bless you Mother and Dad in heaven for helping me have your values to guide my life. I commit to carry forward your legacy of service and pass on your spiritual heritage to my child, Abby.

All My Love, *Dianne*

Contents

KEY SCRIPTURE 13
PREFACE 15
MY STORY 17
BEFORE YOU READ THIS BOOK............................... 23
NEVER TOO LATE 31

Chapter 1 KNOW GOD 35
Chapter 2 STEWARDSHIP 71
Chapter 3 PURITY 99
Chapter 4 KINDNESS 123
Chapter 5 COURAGE 143
Chapter 6 CONFIDENCE 159
Chapter 7 CONVICTION 175
CONCLUSION 197
Postscript IN REMEMBRANCE................................. 205

TRANSFORMATION: Mind—Body—Spirit 207
JOY SCRIPTURES (NIV) 213

DI'S NOVELLA RECIPES 221
MOM'S KEEPER: RELISHES, JAMS AND PICKLES! 223
    SWEET RELISH 225
    CHOW-CHOW RELISH 227
    RHUBARB JAM... 229
    LAZY HOUSEWIFE PICKLES 230
CHICKEN FAMILY FAVORITES 233
    TACO-FLAVORED CHICKEN PLATTER.................. 235
    CHICKEN NICOISE SALAD 237
    CYNCY'S CURRIED CHICKEN SALAD 240

HEAVENLY ANGEL FOODS..243
   MOM'S ANGEL FOOD CAKE....................................245
   GERMAN CHOCOLATE BARS or 2 LAYER CAKE 247
   DI'S FAMOUS CHOCOLATE CAKE..............................250
   14 CARAT CAKE...253
   MOM'S HOMEMADE APPLE CRUMBLE 256
ESCAPADE GALLEY HOLIDAY MEALS 259
   WILDRICE CHICKEN CASSEROLE 261
   CHANTERELLE, PORT & VEAL STEW.........................263
   MOM'S BAKED OYSTER CASSEROLE 266
   DAD'S FAVORITE KOLACHES RECIPE.........................267
LEMON DAYS OF TROUBLE...MAKE LEMON BARS.............269
   LEMON BARS 271

BIBLIOGRAPHY 273
ABOUT DIANNE CONGDON.....................................277
ABOUT "LIVING WATER" ARTIST CAROL CARTER............281

KEY SCRIPTURE

ACTS 2:28 NIV

You have made known to me the paths of life
You will fill me with joy in your Presence.

Stop *running from your fears.*
Seek *the path the Lord has for you.*
Stand *firm to walk in the Joy of Jesus!*

"We are ambassadors of the anointed one who carry the message of Christ to all the world, as though God were tenderly pleading them directly through our lips."

—2 Corinthians 5:20 (TPT)

"Let the hope burst forth within you, releasing a continual joy. Don't give up in a time of trouble, but commune with God at all times."

—Romans 12:12 (TPT)

"The Joy of the Lord is my strength."

—Nehemiah 8:10 (NIV)

"For your very lives are our "letters of recommendations," permanently engraved on our heart, recognized and read by everybody. As a result of our ministry, you are living letters written by Christ, not with ink but by the Spirit of the living God—not carved onto stone tablets but on the tablets of tender hearts."

—2 Corinthians 3: 2-3 (TPT)

PREFACE

The Joy Novella—Recipes for Renewal, was born out of a series of books I authored in the late 1990s with cooking recipes! *The Recipe Novella.* It turned out to be five volumes of recipes collected from my favorite cooking magazines along with my own. I self-published and gave 25 of Volume One for Christmas that year! Such joy! I love reading cookbooks. If you do as well, I think we shall become good friends. Let us cook up something here! When the cooks are in the kitchen, you will find a crowd! These pages will reveal my heart for the Lord! I combine my passions with my God-given purpose: *I exist to serve by Igniting Joy!* I share my innate sense of joy through recipes to restore relationships and transform lives with Our Daily Bread. I invite you to discover ways to reverse feeling hopeless in your life to embracing the Joy of the Lord. The Joy Novella embraces a "never too late" motto of ways to change your thinking and your atmosphere. Finally, enjoy my Chef Notes, gems of wisdom collected over my now 79 young years! Let's *Ignite the Joy of the Lord together.* I invite you to come on in my friend, to come to my table. Have some tea and cake!! Let us *pray through* this thing together. Share your heart with me and, I will share mine. Let us embrace this novella not as fictional prose but perpetual quest to know the reality of the Lord Jesus as our dearest friend and most precious Savior.

MY STORY

Sharing my heart may touch yours to answer the call for a deep and needed healing. My journey helped me bring new life to my marriage with a deeper spiritual understanding. The Lord calls me to view my partner from a higher perspective. He calls me help shift my partner's relationship with the Lord. God has favored me in the calming of my heavy heart with victory through Him. It has caused me to rejoice in how God has used my life's choices to show me His Promises and Blessings. Wasting nothing, the Lord is calling me to blossom spiritually by helping others to awaken! God has called me to share ideas and insights, not to hide from the deep regrets but to embrace them with trust and faith in Him. *The closer we walk, the greater our joy!* It comes from your relationship with the Father's Holy Spirit as His Gift to you. Holy Spirit will show you what next to do.

God wastes nothing. Perhaps and maybe, this will cause you to reconsider everything you, until now, have believed. We put aside the enemy's agenda to reveal God's Plan. Plans to let go and let God help you embrace or release. Some life choices need revisiting with *no they must go*. I don't think of this a just another book on joy. No. I wrote this book to help myself cast to the Christ Mind all that the enemy wanted me to believe was normal. God's joy releases healing to overcome these burdens. Yes, I wrote this book for the Audience of One, my Lord and Savior Jesus Christ. I call it Our Book. I wrote this book to help change my mindset to lean on the Lord rather than my often rehearsed thinking my partner needed changing not me. Thank you, Jesus for showing me a higher perspective. (**Romans 12:2**) Let the Lord go to battle for you while you rest in His Shalom Peace and His Unfailing Love. (**Exodus 14:14**) Be Still. I wrote this to help change lives and release the joy of the Lord over your unbelieving partner or family members. I wrote this to provide tools for becoming a **Joy** Carrier to overcome and transform your relationship with your partner. God is your Heavenly Father in this. Jesus always will be your Spiritual Husband. (**Exodus 1:12**) *You can Count on me to be your Aaron*—holding up your arms!

Join me to know where two or more gather, the Lord resides. (**Matthew 18:20**) This novella honors a vow the Lord gave me. I was reminded of this pain of unequal yoking by the Holy Spirit. Writing about it releases a way to move through it. In this way, the Holy Spirit unleashed my Inner Spirit to let those gifts surface! It is directed as a solution yet, must begin as a foundation to build wisdom and revelation. The Lord alone, instilled me with His **Joy**. Seeing through this lens of joy utterly transformed my perception. Begin to think about how His Healing comes. When might be the last time you were astonished by His Healing Joy? I have learned to separate joy from happiness. Joy remains a constant with the Lord. Happiness comes and, happiness goes depending on the situation. Perhaps you are another one I seek. If you are the one who has been touched by seeking to deepen your joy, then I pray we will become friends. If these healing recipes resonate a difference for you, then I will feel so very blessed. Healing comes when we ask God to search our hearts to know us; test us, He Knows our anxious thoughts. (**Psalm 139:23**) He showed me things to change, as well as to add and beliefs to take away.

Let me clear up any question about who I am. The Holy Spirit is my best friend who gives me wisdom. I deeply love the Lord and give Him all Glory! As my Shepherd, I depend on him to lead me to still waters. Let me also clear up any question of my love for my husband, my life partner, and my friend. Such a beautiful soul with a humble heart. In addition to being faithful, he was very accomplished in business—mentoring many to achieve great success. Bob was a good man who has given me the gift of his love for over 43 years. He was beloved by many. Let there be no question of a life together well lived. This story of my journey includes challenges which causes me to turn to God for help. Every marriage has challenges. I pay it forward, sharing how it has worked for me. How the Lord helps me make these changes. His Presence will prepare the way with guidance for you as well. *What the Lord assigns, He also guides and provides.* We all need the Lord's Holy Spirit Power, Wisdom and Guidance.

I loved my mother's guidance on cooking. With my apron on, I set before me all I need in a clean and clear space. Make sure all the tools are at hand along with the recipe to follow instructions! It occurred to me when the Holy Spirit highlighted this area that I am once again offering a recipe for my future destiny and perhaps yours, as well. Yes, and to follow His commands. How could I know 20+ years ago a God Idea of the Novella would change my life at this time and season? God shows us in part and asks us to trust how it all fits together! Amen! The word Novella describes a short prose tale characterized by teaching and points. Let us help those in unbelief move from doubt to the divinity of the Lord. Jesus brought understanding with simplicity and clarity. He used parables and stories to teach what the Father revealed to Him. The Holy Spirit guided every Word. The Word, backed by the Power of the Almighty Father's Spirit, guided the Lord Jesus during His Earthly teaching. He only spoke what His Father told him to say and did what the Father did. He gave us the Lord's Prayer as simple petitions to the Father. It reveals a blueprint to righteous living. (**Matthew 3:4-19**). The Lord gave us instruction for living, for loving, for forgiving through His

Stories and Parables. I invite you to put on your apron of Jesus protection! Let's get started! Yes! Apron yourself with Jesus.

"It will be good for those servants whose master finds them watching when he comes. Truly I tell you, he will dress himself to serve, (apron) will have them recline at the table and will come and wait on them."

—Luke 12:37 (NIV)

Let's face it, some days we need to put on the apron and bake a cake and eat it too! Every relationship can have difficulties that test us. How we view them all makes the difference. Let us be encouraged in solving our approach to find solutions through the lens of **Joy**. **Joy**, without question, will change the atmosphere! Being a **Joy** Carrier becomes a Godly Blessing to transform whatever shows up. It causes us to drop all pretenses about our identity. The Lord already knows your everything. Be honest with yourself and with Him. Let us prepare for a move of God in our lives, putting *God First* in all our experiences. Let us seek God's Peace to replace and restore the issues that can divide us. Let us understand what the enemy is trying to do in our lives. Let us take a journey to imagine what can occur to affect a shift. Let us sift and shift our thinking to bring us freedom from any pain. Let us bake a cake to celebrate Christ being in us. It expresses God's glorious revelation for a Cake of Joy rather than a cake of regrets. Our cake will be called a Cake of Hope and Glory! Some days we need to apron ourselves with Jesus, become humble and let go of the rest.

Carefully blend in Christ's Ways then, fold into our batter the Power of His Living Word to bring us strength. Please, do not forget the salt to savor the flavor. We are the Salt and the Light! Finally, we are ready to add the most generous gift of the Lord, His Unfailing Love to the pan, bake and *Wait on the Lord*. We let the Lord bake in the elements of His

Presence to restore any issues of unbelief or doubt. We *Wait on the Lord* for His Revelation giving us wisdom and a new vision for our lives. We open our hearts to hear His Voice. His Breath moves over us, in us and, through us. Now is the time to fix our eyes on the Lord. We help each other to stay awake while the cake is baking! We give each other encouragement with Hope and Glory of the Holy Spirit from the Lord as our Baker Advocate. Let us seek the scriptures to discover the recipes of the Lord.

Imagine The Joy Novella restoring your hope to make a heavy heart sing once again! Only the Lord can remove discouragement. With His Clarity and Focus, He transforms your life to be His Blessing for your marriage partners, your children, family members, neighbors, and friends. His Blessing to bring your partner to believe and know Him. Choosing to walk in the Spirit of the Lord will shift all these relationships. He helps open the doors to healing the unbelief of our partner. Seeking counsel from the Lord will show us His Amazing Love is unfailing. Nothing is impossible for Jesus. Clarity on this will help you please God with making Him First in all things, above all else. His Favor will come over you and bless your barns. His Powerful Healing Presence will build the necessary foundation for families, marriages, and friendships to withstand the storms. Through faith, we can better handle the storms of life. Arguments tend to deposit debris. Removing those things that block a clear path to the Lord helps to create a beautiful foundation. Then adding prayer, trust and faith restores the **Joy** in renewing our hearts with love to bear fruit. All of these come together when you walk with the Holy Spirit. It comforts you with a Triune God Blessing (**Ecclesiastes 4:12**) over your life. You are qualified, my friend, to step into your power, the Power of the Holy Spirit.

BEFORE YOU READ THIS BOOK

WHAT YOU NEED BEFORE YOU READ:

- **A Prayer Journal** to record your reflections and declarations.

- **An Idea Journal** to carry with you to record creative things God wants you to do.

- **A Sacred Time** in a **Sacred Altar Place** to worship and reflect.

- **A Spiritual Altar** set aside in your home where you connect with the Lord.

The Lord has called you for a purpose. *Consider who He calls you to be, to embrace and to know.* You are a chosen one. One who is blessed. Yes, anointed. One who is ready to answer the call. You are called a Follower of the Lord. *Go forth to embrace this mission with me.* You are qualified.

Repeat each one: *I am called to know…God calls me to walk with…He calls to equip me as a…He calls me to be…*

GODLY GLOSSARY

Eternal Father God-Yahweh: Abba (Daddy)-One True Living God of all Creation, The Most High God, The Just and Righteous Judge, Jehovah Elohim, Supreme Authority

Ye-shua Hamashiach-Messiah: Hebrew for the Lord Jesus Christ, the Only Begotten Son of the Father God, King of Glory, King of the Jews

Lord Je-sus Christ-Messiah: Son of God, The Perfector of Faith, Living Word, Our Daily Bread, Living Torah, Anointed Deliverer, King of the Jews

Mel-chiz-e-dek: The King of Salem, High Priest of the Order of Melchizedek who blessed Abraham. **Genesis14:18**, Without a Father and Mother

A-bra-ham: The Father of all the Nations. **Genesis 17:5-7**

A-bide: To wait patiently for

Ab-ne-gate: To deny to oneself; give up or renounce

A-lign-ment: To be in line with Kingdom Principals

A-men: to express and end a prayer with conviction with complete trust

A-pron: a garment worn to protect one's clothes; to protect, provide a covering

As-cribe: To attribute to a specific source or origin

A-ston-ish-ing: To fill with sudden wonder or amazement; a marvel

Au-da-cious: Fearlessly daring; boldness, to be eager

A-wak-en-ing: The act of waking; emergence from sleep

Bi-ble: The Living Word summed up as: Love God and Love God's People

Bless-ing: To invoke God's Divine Favor over a person, a thing, a place, a nation

Chef: a cook, especially the chief cook of a large kitchen, guardianship

Cher-ish: To hold dear; treat with tenderness and affection

Chief: The one highest in authority; a leader; Creative Spiritual Authority

Cho-sen: Selected from or preferred above others

Cit-i-zen: A person owing loyalty to what governs them

Con-form: To come to have the same form / act in agreement / be in accord

Con-quer-or: To overcome; to be victorious

Cook-er-y: The art or practice of preparing food, your Daily Bread

Cov-e-nant: By words, a solemn agreement between God and His People

Cov-e-nant: God's Promises to man as recorded in the Old and New Testament

De-liv-er-ance: Delivering from bondage or danger

Dis-cern-ment: To perceive, to detect something obscure or hidden

Dis-ci-pline: Training, a specified character, pattern or improvement

Dun-a-mis: A Greek word for Holy Spirit Power, Father God's Spiritual Power

Ec-cle-si-a: An assembly to carry the Mantle of God's Voice and Authority

E-pis-tle: An Apostle in the New Testament, A carrier of the Word, Ambassador

Faith: Belief and trust in God; loyalty, belief in truth, value, person, idea, or thing.

Fol-low-er: One that comes after another, a pursuer, a servant, a disciple

Food: Anything that nourishes or sustains physically or spiritually

For-give: To excuse for a fault; to pardon; to absolve from payment

Glo-ry: Exalted honor, praise, adoration, majestic beauty, and splendor

Ho-ly: Worthy of worship, revered high esteem, sacred divine power

Hon-or: Esteem, respect, reverence; glory, nobility of mind; gesture of blessing

Im-por-tune: State of being insistent, persistent

In-ter-cep-tion: Intercept with a blessing; mediation; Divine Protection

Joy: A feeling or high pleasure or delight; happiness, gladness

King-dom: The eternal spiritual sovereignty of God

Kitch-e-ner: 1 A kitchen manager (especially in a monastery)

Kitch-en: The place of gathering to prepare foods, a cook's domain

Lamb: The Lamb of God; a member of the flock

Love: Devotion to God, intense affection concerning another

Meek: Showing patience and humility; long-suffering

No-vel-la: A prose tale; characterized being short and to the point

Of-fer-ing: A presentation made to God as an act of worship

Pi-o-neer: A trailblazer, an innovator, a foot solider sent to clear the way

Priesthood: A Royal Priesthood in the Order of Melchizedek

Re-born: Born from Above spiritually, emotionally, revived and renewed

Re-buke: To criticize, to scold sharply, or reprimand

Rec-i-pe: Set of instructions; directions; a formula for preparing foods

Re-cip-i-ence The capacity to receive; receptivity

Re-cip-i-ent: One who receives or is receptive

Rec-on-cile: To re-establish friendship between; settle or resolve a dispute

Re-pent-ance: Remorse or contrition for past conduct or sin

Res-o-lute: Showing determination; unwavering; a fixed purpose; faithful

Sal-va-tion: Redemptive deliverance of man's soul with Blood of Lamb

Sanc-ti-ty: Godliness, sacredness

Scrip-ture: A sacred writing in the Bible, the Holy Scripture

She-ki-nah: a visible manifestation of the divine presence of the Holy Spirit

Shep-herd: One who cares for His Sheep; One who cares for His Followers

Shift: To change position or direction; manage an outcome or to overcome

Sift: Using a device to separate the fine from the coarse in order to refine

Stat-ure: A level achieved; status

Stead-fast: Firmly loyal or constant, unswerving, faithful

Sub-mis-sion: To yield; to surrender to the will of another

Su-per-nat-u-ral: Attributed to the exercise of Divine Power

Sur-ren-der: To relinquish possession or control

Thanks-giv-ing: An act of expressing gratitude and thanks especially to God

T.H.G.A.T.G.: To Him Give All Th Glory

Tithe: gifts to honor the King and His Kingdom; worship, gifts of worth

To-rah: Father God's Ways and Teachings, not law, first 5 books in Bible

Tri-une: Being three in one, Godhead of the Trinity, a trinity

Trust-wor-thy: Warranting trust; dependable; reliable; trustworthiness

Un-be-lief: Lack of belief or faith, especially in spiritual matters

Un-e-qual: Being unmatched, ill-matched, having unbalanced parts

Wis-dom: Understanding of what is true, right or lasting

Yok-ed: To connect, to join or to bind together

"As for me and my household we will serve the Lord."

—Joshua 24:15 (NIV)

"A person may have many ideas concerning God's plan for his life but only the designs of God's purpose will succeed in the end."

—Proverbs 19:23 (TPT)

NEVER TOO LATE

MY UNFOLDING JOURNEY

At age 75, being Born from Above by the Holy Spirit was astonishing! It helped me turn the tables on understanding my partner. It came about from two decisions I made that changed my life entirely. My sister-in-law encouraged me to consider Mentoring with James Goll. I, for sure, needed a mentor. As a result, I joined the Empower 2000 Family of Dr. Joseph Peck for Spirit-Filled Webinars pouring forth like a spiritual faucet. One class led to the next. In the spring of 2018, The Dove Baptism brought to me comfort, assurance, and awareness of the Promises of the Lord. Next, a course on Hearing God's Voice with Mark Virkler's Ministry opened the world of the Holy Spirit anointing with two significant visions. I rejoice at His Presence to bring me this understanding. These visions solidly placed me on my path with Yeshua. I sought time alone with the Lord to hear from Him. Holy Spirit began to awaken me in the night hours to sit with the Lord. One night, *a bright light* moved all around me. The more I would look up, the greater I felt the Lord's Presence. I took these moments very seriously. My trust in the Holy Advocate deepened. Now, I seek Him daily to fellowship with Him. Now, Holy Spirit Guides my everything. I am careful not to overbook a day to allow time for Holy Spirit Margins needed for prayers and unexpected tasks. I ask and wait for Him to direct and conduct me. I am quick to obey Him. Holy Spirit leads my life. Most importantly, the Holy Spirit helps me love more deeply my husband, my family, my friends, and every single person on my path. Holy Spirit helps me see the Astonishing Joy in all things. It gives me such encouragement and hope. I live in expectation to joyfully enlarge my purpose and identity in the Lord.

"I have made you known to them, and will continue to make you known in order that the love you have for me may be in them and that I myself may be in them."

—John 17:26 (NIV) *The Lord prays for His Disciples*

"May the God of hope fill you with all joy and peace as you trust in him, so that you may overflow with the hope by the power of the Holy Spirit."

—Romans 15:13 (NIV)

"For I know the plans I have for you." Declares the Lord, "plans to prosper you and not to harm you, plans to give you hope and a future. Then you will call on me and come and pray to me and I will listen to you. You will seek me and find me when you seek me with all your heart."

—Jeremiah 29:11-13 (NIV)

"And those he predestined, he also called; those he called, he also justified and those he justified, he also glorified."

—Romans 8:30 (NIV)

I also love the TPT version of this. Permit me to share it as well:

"Having determined our destiny time ahead of, he called us to himself and transferred his perfect righteousness he co-glorified with his Son."

—**Romans 8:30** (TPT) *Praise the Lord!*

Finally, Joy Novella offers a what-if solution. *What if He rendered your heart like the early Kansas pioneers to walk with Him in a new and tender way?* *What if you found a new and higher understanding of how God goes to battle on your behalf? What if a new mindset would shift your entire life?* The battles belong to the Lord, so unexpected attacks or occurrences do not shake me, nor does it shake my resolve. (**2 Chronicles 20:15**) Mine is to love and the Lord to restore. As Prophet Bob Jones, before graduating to heaven, asked of his close circle: "Have you learned to love?" I am obeying the Lord with love for the lessons of my circumstances. The Lord seeks through the destinies of each one of us to *Restore the Kingdom* with our talents, gifts, and circumstances. Let each of us on our journey be *Sold Out* for Jesus! Let our walk be astonishing with Him! The Lord is doing a *New Creation* through us! (**2 Corinthians 5:17**)

With my journey, I have learned God wastes nothing. The fact that the word **joy** is found in the NIV Bible 218 times tells me **JOY** is a high priority for the Lord God. Only through God can you attain fullness of **joy**! My Prayer rests for you and me to have our portion! (**Psalm 73:26**) May His Strength be our **joy**! God loves us and wants us safe, protected, with provision for all we need to walk with Him. The Lord turns everything into good. So let us open the space in our mind to be clear what is ideal for our Cake of Hope and Glory. Let the Lord's Prayer be our guide. *Each petition of the Lord's Prayer offers a step to become a reflection for our beloveds. We walk as a modeled example for the Body of Christ.* (**Matthew**

6:9-13) The **Chef Notes** add some wit and wisdom to make this a good and satisfying meal to read!

"For the battle is not yours, but God's."

—2 Chronicles 20:15 (NIV)

"So, we are convinced that every detail of our lives is continually woven together for good, for we are his lovers who have been called to fulfill his designed purpose."

—Romans 8:2 (TPT)

"I am the way and the truth and the life. No one comes to the Father except through me. If you really KNOW me, you will KNOW my Father as well. From now on you do KNOW him and have seen him."

—John 14:6-7 (NIV)

Chapter 1

KNOW GOD

Our Father Which Art in Heaven; Hallowed be they Name.

SIFT AND SHIFT YOUR LIFE WITH KNOWING— MAKING GOD A PRIORITY.

CHEF NOTE: One usually knows the outcome or reason when heading to the kitchen. Cook, eat, and come together. Hey, the kitchen is where the family gathers! Good cooks begin with outcomes. They see the finished dish ahead of time. The ability to see ahead of time helps to prepare a delicious meal. First, gather the essentials needed, invented or otherwise! Not long ago, I was remembering a time when my mother needed something for her recipe from the *root cellar*. Oh, the root cellar memories! As a little girl, I played on our cellar door! You remember that song: *Say Say Playmates!* Come slide down my cellar door! The door was angled to accommodate the steep stairs! I loved to lie on the door! The cellar was also a place of safe keeping when Kansas tornadoes descended from the dark skies! Most of all, the cellar became my mother's *keeper!* All the summer's canning along with the root veggies were down there. A large vat of sauerkraut was always brewing down there for Dad! Mom's staples were there for the cooking needs. She could take a mere nothing and multiply it into a delicious something! Born in 1906, that's what pioneer women did.

Wherever Jesus went, a crowd gathered. They were thirsty and hungry for Him. Through Yeshua, the Father multiplied five fishes and two loaves (**John 3:16**) to feed the thousands who came to hear him preach on the Mount of Olives. He fed them spiritually and physically. He offers reassurance through his Daily Bread. Yeshua became the Living Word for the Father's People. Jesus became our Savior and the Father's Plan for Salvation. Jesus was born to reveal the Father. He taught the disciples how to know the Father God and Love God's People. He came to earth as a Son of Man to bring God's Salvation through His Shed Blood to the Jewish people. Jesus was given authority over all heaven and on earth to send His eleven followers for His Great Commission. He instructed them to go and make disciples of all nations, baptizing them in the Name of the Father and the Son and of the Holy Spirit and teaching them to obey His Commandments. (**Matthew 28:19**) Later, the Lord converted the Apostle Paul to minister to churches of the gentiles. My great commission addresses unequal yoking from a higher perspective for unions to be blessed. As His Bride, we are all called (commissioned) to disciple wherever we are planted. We belong to Him through the Resurrection Power of the Cross. The Lord Jesus Christ is our *keeper*. Jesus is our *Promise Keeper, Way Maker, and Light in the Darkness.*

"I, the Lord, watch over it; I water it continually I guard it day and night so that no one may harm it."

—**Isaiah 27:3** (NIV) The Father is continually keeping.

"Lord, the God of Israel there is no God like you in heaven above or on earth below—you who keep your covenant love with your servants who continue wholeheartedly in your way."

—1 Kings 8:23 (NIV) The Father keeps His Covenant.

"For it is God who works in you to will and to act in order to fulfill his good purpose."

—Philippians 2: 13 (NIV) The Father keeps me absolutely.

"This is what I covenanted with you when you came out of Egypt, and my spirit remains among you. Do not fear."

—Haggai 2:5 (NIV) The Father keeps His Covenant. Never break a covenant with God.

"If you love me, keep my commands."

—John 14:15 (NIV) Be in obedience to the Father's Commandments.

"The Lord bless you and KEEP you; the Lord make his face shine on you and be gracious to you; the Lord turn his face toward you and give you peace."

—Numbers 6:24-26 (NIV) The Lord is your Keeper.

Rend the heart with pioneer joy! The Joy of the Lord is a remarkable gift to the heart. This gift opens the heart afresh every morning to sweep in His Glory! His strength creates my joy! The Strength of the Lord rescued my weakness as I sought to *know* Him. In addition to meditation and prayer, I began turning to Yeshua for small chats and long walks. Singing and stargazing in the darkness of early mornings. (Yes, a Morning Girl.) My house awakened before dawn. I grew up in a small Czechoslovakian Kansas community just off dead center of the United States. Holyrood exudes Midwestern hometown goodness. After my parents were Called Home to the Lord, I still loved going home as often as possible. One year my brother and I returned to Holyrood for a High School Reunion. The Saturday morning parade featured kids on bikes, tractors, fire trucks, horses, and all manner of small-town sweetness. A dear friend of my brother's invited us to his very vast farm to see a homesteaded original *sod house*. Tucked away from the Kansas winds in a grove of trees and grasses stood this monument to bravery. Yes, an earthen home built by courageous pioneers whose hearts surely were led by the Lord. With perseverance, they followed their *inner vision* from God. In faith, they came aboard ships to flee a dark past seeking freedom to worship and acquire land to create their destiny. Imagine having only candles and the sun to light their way. Yes, they give their hearts to the Lord for His Light to shine on their darkness. Imagine Kansas winters. We stood there in amazement that it remained to this day as a testimony to God's strength given to a pioneering spirit. They were filled with *faith* following their innate belief and trust in God's Power to deliver them. Imagine, leaving your land of origin to build a new life in an unknown destination. Think about the Faith. (**1 Corinthians 2:5**) Think of the surrender it took to trust the Lord and His Promises. It is a lesson for all of us that through surrender you will be blessed. Let us all have a pioneer mindset to seek the Lord with all our hearts and souls. Let us all have the courage to embark on a new thing or take a stand for a cause! It was stunning to see the sacrifice they made for freedom to worship God. I needed to be open to the Lord's desire for my next steps. This meant time alone.

"Rend your heart and not your garments. Return to the Lord you God, for he is gracious and compassionate, slow to anger and abounding in love, and he relents from sending calamity."

—Joel 2:12 (NIV)

"And let us run with perseverance the race marked out for us, fixing our eyes on Jesus, the pioneer and perfecter of faith."

—Hebrews 12:1-2 (NIV)

Decide now to make time for the Lord. Making time alone with Yeshua resets my joy in my heart each morning. It requires discipline to say no to the flesh and a yes to the Lord. A no to the world for a yes to Eternal Life. Saying yes means carving out time for Him. I go to bed early to arise with the birds! I find 4 to 6 a.m. to be quiet and the most productive hours in my day. The Father God loves order and discipline. What you do in the natural translates to the spiritual outcome. The natural must always come first.

I remember visiting my daughter in Paris in the 80s. She enrolled in a semester abroad program to study French. I discovered Paris never sleeps. Never was there a quiet moment. Think back to the sod house with Holy Spirit winds blowing accompanied by howling wolves. *Carve out undisturbed* time for Him. Settle into a rhythm of quiet with Him. Do not be in a hurry. Become disciplined for Him. Seek Him first. (**Matthew 6:33**). The more time I *devoted to Him*, the *greater His Presence* came to me. Thus, my day begins with fixing my eyes on Jesus to know the Father, Jehovah Elohim, my Abba Daddy Father, my Dwelling Place of the Most High, and Papa. Only through the Son, Jesus, can we know the Father. Only through the Holy Spirit, the Spirit of the Father God who is an actual person, can we know Jesus-Yeshua, our Savior.

(**John 6:63**) Before going to bed, I ask the Lord for a Proverbs Scripture during the night or to give me dreams or visions of what He wants me to know. Be proactive to fellowship with the Jesus. Upon arising, I begin my day with His Presence, and His Living Word.

Know the Father through Jesus, the Living Word. (**John 1:14**) *He is the Word made flesh. We must be willing and make ourselves available to be in relationship with Jesus.* This allows His Holy Spirit to stir your heart to yearn for Him. There was a time I thought *feeling* led to knowing and understanding something. Feeling the Presence assures me God shows me the way. What about when you don't feel the Presence? It is like falling in love with someone with your heart, putting the mind's need to know on the back burner. Only intimacy of His Word will bring you knowing. Think back to falling in love the first time was probably based on feeling. 'Yet, it took years to know. The Father God sent His Spirit to help us *know the ways* of Jesus. (**Acts 2:2-4**) Through immersing oneself in communion with the Holy Spirit we will know the Lord. We must give the Holy Spirit a place of honor in our daily lives. The teachings of Jesus came from the Father who sent Him. (**John 7:16**). Jesus surrendered to the Father's Will only doing with the Father did. The Father's Spirit comes to remind us of Jesus's teachings and commands while on earth. Holy Spirit directs the work of the Lord. The Holy Spirit is necessary as out guide. (**Galatians 5:25**) During my *Born from Above* time, the Presence was daily wooing me with visions. These visions allowed me to move from feeling about Jesus from a distance to *knowing Him intimately* as my *Savior*. (**Exodus 33:13**) Then, a deep friendship followed. It is up to me to create time to learn to know the Lord, making Him my priority. He offers the promise of the hope of our calling and the riches of our inheritance when we do our part. (**Ephesians 1:17-19**) Seeking Him reveals how you will know Him. Intimacy reveals unsearchable knowledge. Intimacy releases wisdom through signs and wonders, all of which bring such Joy when seeking

His Face. This joy then ushers in His Gift of the Holy Spirit Advocate. Oh, it is *Astonishing how it all works for His Glory!*

"If you are pleased with me, teach me your ways so I may KNOW you and continue to find favor with you."

—Exodus 33:13 (NIV)

"I am the way and the truth and the life. No one comes to the Father except through me. If you really want to KNOW me, you will KNOW my Father as well. From now on, you do KNOW him ad have seen him."

—John 14:6-7 (NIV)

"Give God the right to direct your life, and as you trust him along the way, you'll find he pulled it off perfectly!"

—Psalm 37:5 (TPT)

"I want to KNOW Christ—yes, to know the power of his resurrection and participation in his sufferings, becoming like him in his death, and so somehow attaining to the resurrection from the dead."

—Philippians 3:10-11 (NIV)

"To truly KNOW Him meant letting go of everything from my past and throwing all my boasting on the garbage heap. It's all like a pile of manure to me now, so that I may be enriched in the reality of knowing Jesus Christ and embrace him as Lord in all of His greatness."

—Philippians 3:8 (TPT)

"God said to Moses, "I AM WHO I AM." This is what you are to say to the Israelites: I AM has sent me to you."

—Exodus 3:13 (NIV)

Let's go back to Mom's Kitchen. Take my love of cooking, for example. It started in our kitchen in Holyrood, Kansas, with my mentor mother, who canned and cooked in humility for us. Next, my high school required Home Economics which, among other things, included cooking. I know this is not the way of today, yet, bear with me. I recently went through my Mother's Recipe box to discover my high school cooking class cards! My first cookbook was Betty Crocker. Whatever happened to Betty anyway?

My mother-in-law, Milly, taught me things. She was a shoot-from-the-hip type of cook! My first cooking classes began at the Pampered Pantry in St. Louis, Missouri. I spent a year with Chef Jean Pierre Auge studying French Cuisine. That recipe collection went into a 3-inch binder of gathered treasures. I studied cooking fundamentals and attended special classes with Chef Jean Pierre's Cooking School in Ft. Lauderdale. To this day, I never stop learning new things. It is the same way in truly seeking the Father. Begin by making Jesus your best friend.

Seek the Living Word to Know the Father. Jesus *never stops* revealing himself *when we seek Him*. The greater our seeking, the more near He draws to us. When you love and enjoy something, you become intimate with learning about that something. Learning opens your pathway to knowing. Knowing is the foundation for gaining authority. Authority comes from knowing Yeshua as the Living Word. This Living Word is found in the first five books of the bible called the Torah, the Hebrew word for instruction. (**Psalm 32:8**) All the remaining parts of the bible contain the seeds of God's Instruction found in the Torah. With all authority over all in heaven and on earth, Yeshua reveals how each of us can intimately know His Father. (**Matthew 28:18**) Only through the Son, Jesus, can we know Eternal Life with the Father. The Living Word aprons us with His Unfailing Love Promises. (**Psalm 143:10**) Now is the time to put on your apron, friends!

"How blessed are the servants whom the master finds watching for him when he comes! I tell all of you with certainty, he himself will put on an apron, make them sit down at the table, and go around and serve them."

—Luke 12:37 (ISV)

Study more to know more. In her *Women of the Word*, Jen Wilkin advises studying the bible with both the heart and the mind. If you are seeking to know God's Word, I highly recommended her book. She reveals her most important understanding of moving from loving God with her heart to knowing God with her mind. She grew into her knowing with her need to grow in the knowledge of the *I AM*. She shares, "People ask me, how do you get more pleasure out of life?" My answer is extremely pedantic: *"study more."* She expresses, "The heart cannot love what the mind does not know." (**Proverbs 19:27**) I am reminded of wanting to play the violin that was in my mother's family.

There was no one to teach me. Dreams of playing a violin came to me around age 10 or 11. Never did I let go of this dream. Finally, after turning 50, I rented a violin and found a teacher who would take on an adult (God Bless Him). Next, the humbling Suzuki lessons with young, gifted six-year-olds, revealing impressive talents. Finally, a Russian teacher took me under his wing. Not only did I somewhat flourish, Eddy got me into the Hallandale Symphony Orchestra. Just imagine it! Only God can make the impossible possible! Naturally, my position was the end of the line in 2nd violins as the page-turner. I was a very reliable and good page-turner! I turned with ease and on time! I grew into my role there because I rehearsed daily for every concert. I was determined to elevate my dream as a child become a reality. I realized my knowing came through discipline to read the Word as I continued to live out this miracle! I urge you to begin now to know the *"I AM* Father" with all your heart to grow spiritually through the study of His Word. Each day we are given hours to *birth knowing.* Use them wisely. Make the Word a priority.

"God said to Moses, "I AM WHO I AM." This is what you are to say to the Israelites: I AM has sent me to you."

—Exodus 3:13 (NIV)

As a newborn Believer, you are God's Priority. *Make knowing Papa your priority. Then you will awaken to know the Lord God is your life.* (**Deuteronomy 30:20**) All things originate from the Father. We are His Children. He sees each of us as perfect and complete. This includes our partners and families. His Love never stops loving. His Love for each of us will remain long after words of knowledge are forgotten. (**1 Corinthians 13:8-9**) If you are a parent, you will recall the early attention needed for helping a newborn flourish into the later years. Well, you are the Lord's *newborn.* He never leaves you unattended. He knows what you need. As you grow in your devotion and worship, His Faithfulness reveals how much He Cares. He loves you no matter what you do. He will never forsake or leave you. (**Hebrews 13:5**) His very Presence drives away our fears replacing them steadfastly with His Joy and His Presence.

Pause now and recall the number of times the Lord saved you from disaster. Say, *"Thank you, Jesus!"* I recall being a mother for the first time. I read one time, a birth of a baby is also the birth of a mother. How true! My instincts were always on high alert being a new mother. I recall my toddler sitting in her little walker at the top of the stairs with me at the bottom. *Oh Lord, help me.* My precious Abby. I keep an old billfold with her baby and school pictures handy. Whenever I need a lift, I open it up and look at the radiance of her face. *Joy* shows up. Yeshua teaches us to care deeply for His Children. (**1John 3:1**) See what great love the Father has lavished on us that we should be called Children of God. As His Children we must not be led astray. Whoever does what is right is *righteous.*

"Can a mother forget the baby at her breast and have no compassion on the child she has borne? Though she may forget, I will not forget you! See, I have engraved you on the palms of my hands; your walls are ever before me."

—Isaiah 49:15-16 (NIV)

Pursue, practice, and discern righteousness. The Lord has engraved you on the Palm of His Hand. (**Isaiah 49:16**) He watches over you as His Anointed One. His Holy Spirit reveals your right from wrong actions. Then the Holy Spirit will show you the way to go through the Word. The scriptures are here to *train* you in the path of righteousness. (**2 Timothy 3:16**) Dr. Jeff Hazim of Kingdom Embassy Ministries teaches to understand righteousness begins by *pursuing* righteousness. Do what the Lord God Commands us to do. Seek to be Born from Above by the Holy Spirit Baptism. Holy Spirit becomes our guide to righteousness. Righteousness will determine how each of us will be judged. (**2 Corinthians 5:21**) Therefore, pursue righteousness to become worthy and remain upright in your heart. Next, *practice* righteousness through His Commands. Stepping away from the instruction of the Father equates to sin. Sin no more.

Finally, *discern* righteousness by walking closely with Yeshua to know His Ways. Walk in righteousness to remain in Him. (**Philippians 4:9**) He wants us to put into practice what we have learned. He taught us to pause often and seek Him to enlighten our hearts. He wants us alert to those who deny Him. He wants to protect us against the enemy who sets out to destroy us. As His Sheep, He tends to our hurts and wants us filled with His Peace. He Shepherds and Leads us watching for the strays. (**Psalm 23:1-2**) His Holy Spirit guides us to remember Yeshua's commands. He wants each of us to do what He does, just as He did only what the Father told Him to do and say and be. The Father God sent His Only Begotten Son to us as a Plan for Salvation. *Only through Jesus* can we know the Father to gain Eternal Life. (**John 14:6**) Christ walked in humility doing His Father's Will delivered by the Holy Spirit Power who helps us pursue, practice, and discern right from wrong. (**Psalm 34:5**) Walking in righteousness establishes the justice of the Father. He will hear your cry! Mature believers are called to follow the Father's Mercy through the Holy Spirit Power. His Spirit helps us have clean hands to grow stronger. (**Job 17:9**) We want this Holy Spirit Power to come alive in our beloveds.

"For everyone who knows your wonderful name keeps putting their trust in you. They can count on you for help no matter what."

—Psalms 9:10 (TPT)

Come alive with the Holy Spirit Power! In the beginning, God created the heavens and the earth. Then he said, *"Let us make mankind in our image and likeness."* The Trinity of God is our creator! (Genesis 1:26) Th Holy Spirit carries the mighty Power of God, the Father, and the Son as the third person of the Godhead, carries the Father's Authority Holy Spirit acts as a co-equal with the Father and the Son in which he carries the Father's Power. All three of the Godhead are co-equals being *omnipresent, omnipotent, and omniscient* and able to search the Mind of the Father. Become immersed in the Holy Spirit Power who is all-knowing like the Father and Son. Only through the Holy Spirit Power will you know the Father and the Son. The more deeply you know the Holy Spirit the more you will know Jesus. It is essential to make the Holy Spirit your best friend and dearest companion. Satan gave up his authority when he crucified Jesus on the cross. He never can be all-present, nor have all-power nor all-knowing. Holy Spirit protects against the evil one. The moment you surrender to Yeshua/Jesus, He will send you His Holy Spirit. We want our beloveds in total protection. (**2 Corinthians 3:17**) Day by day we seek renewal for them through prayer to surrender to the Lord. When your partner gives his heart to the Lord and surrenders, this becomes a Covenant with God. (**Hebrews 13:20-21**) The great Shepherd will equip your beloved just as he equips you with everything good for doing His Will. God works by Covenant to bring the Holy Spirit to be His Messenger within your heart. Day by Day the Holy Spirit empowers us with His Gifts.

"And now, because we are united to Christ we both have equal and direct access in the realm of the Holy Spirit to come before the Father."

—Ephesians 2:18 (TPT)

Holy Spirit brings His Gifts. Fruits and Gifts of the Holy Spirit give us a foundation in Christ. (**Galatians.5:22**) This becomes a foundation for our relationship with our family and especially our beloved partner. When you are working through issues with your partner, these gifts become valuable tools. As you read below, ask yourself are you being a gift to your partner? I recall as a little girl being all alone in front bedroom which was wall-papered with roses. There was one rose at eye level that was special. I would lay on my side and talk with this rose, probably about things. Little did I realize I was already meeting with

Jesus and His Holy Spirit. Those little talks were so comforting. So, walking in the Spirit means the Holy Spirit will comfort you to remember what Jesus needs you to do and be. Only when Jesus went to be at the Right Hand of the Father did the Power of the Father's Holy Spirit come to the disciples. As we embrace the Father's Spirit, we can truly become intimate with the Son, Jesus, to experience His Love. The Father God and Lord Jesus sent the Holy Spirit to continue to teach what Jesus taught on earth. He lives within us as the Comforter, the Helper, and the Advocate. (**John 14:15-16**) Jesus promised the Spirit of the Father that you would not become an orphan. Forty Days after Jesus death, He ascended to heaven. Ten days later, the Holy Spirit descended upon the waiting disciples (**Acts 2:2-4**) All of them were filled with the Holy Spirit and began speaking in other tongues. All the people had assembled from all the nations and were astounded to hear their own language all declaring the wonders of God.

The Language of the Spirit comes from being baptized in the Holy Spirit. As you deepen your walk with the Lord the Holy Spirit will gift you with His Blessings. Speaking in tongues is one of them. We speak in tongues for spiritual guidance, spiritual warfare, deepen our Inner Spirit Man, and allow the Holy Spirit to present our prayers to the Father, especially when we are not sure what or how to pray. He is continually guiding our thoughts and actions. His Conviction occurs when we step off our path. We must repent and confess. At the same time, we use the authority of Yeshua to rebuke the enemy's strongholds of darkness. (**2 Corinthians 10:5**) Lastly, give praise knowing the Father forgives us. His great gifts inspire us to discern righteousness, right from wrong, good from evil. The Holy Spirit uses our prayers to help our partners deal with the enemy.

Recognize the enemy. It is imperative to awaken to how Satan, the enemy has led us astray with his lies. Why? The agent of darkness loves to come through your partner to get to you! He loves a house divided against itself. Realize a person living in unbelief of the Father God is subject to the influence of evil. This is how depression sets in backed by despair. (**Ephesians 2:1-2**) This is all about obedience. **Matthew 12:43-45** helps us become aware why the Gifts of the Spirit are essential to prevent the enemy to have influence over us. Wisdom, Understanding and Knowledge of the Father is our protection. This understanding changes how we can view our partners. I began to see the lies of the enemy fostered many issues. Here is where the Holy Spirit steps in to assist us. The more awake we become, the easier we feel the needed conviction. The Holy Spirit becomes our Triune experience of the Father Abba and Son Jesus. Therefore, to become the Image of Christ, we must immerse ourselves in the Holy Spirit. This creates the foundation for spiritual growth filled with trust and faith. Holy Spirit Gifts are given to help us remember what the Lord taught us while on earth. That is why your body temple houses the Holy Spirit. Has the Holy Spirit come to baptize you with His Holy Spirit Fire? The Holy Spirit helps to reverse a life filled with doubts and death into being filled with faith, hope and life.

"…Any kingdom divided against itself will be ruined, and any house divided against itself will fall."

—Luke 11:17 (NIV)

Hope comes from faith and trust in Spirit of the Father. It seems we live in a hopeless world. I often think back to my childhood years. I so loved growing up in Kansas simplicity. When I was probably 10 years old, my dad built a small house behind the garage near the sidewalk that led to the alley. I watched with interest as windows were cut out and little flower boxes were added. A tool shed sweetheart, was the answer to what he was building. It turned out to be my birthday present—my very own playhouse. It had rafters and a wooden floor. I had a chair and a table. All I needed was a bed and I would live here I thought. I loved my house that Dad built. It became my safe haven.

You see it is the same with the house built by our Father's Son, Jesus, our Rock. (**Matthew 7:24**) You become His House. You are His Tabernacle of Light. Your body becomes a temple (**1 Corinthians 6:19-20**). Honor God with your temple. His House protects our tender souls from the storms. You must not watch the storm as it robs your faith. It is not wise to lean on your own understanding. (**Proverbs 3:5**) When we walk in the Spirit, we are trusting in the Unseen Reality of the Lord. The Lord anoints us with His Life. When you focus on the world's chaos, walking by sight, it produces despair and even fear. Become the one to bring hope to others, especially your partner. Make the Lord the Anchor of your Soul. (**Hebrews 6:19**) Choosing hope connects faith to His Love which brings healing to the heart. (**Jeremiah 29:11**) Because you are a Carrier of Hope, others might ask why are you so hopeful? Let the Love of the Lord be your calling card! Call upon the Name of Jesus! His Name is to be Sanctified. (**Philippians 2:9-10**) Become His Astonishing Joy Carrier as well! *Let this calling card open the eyes of your partner!* They will begin to realize, by your Love, you walk with the Lord. (**1 John 4:15-16**) Then, you will become known by the Love of the Lord you carry. You will "radiate" with the Hope of the Lord's Glory! Truly, you have Jesus on your side! Make time for Him. His Love for you is beyond your comprehension. To Know Him is to Worship Him.

"But the fruit of the Spirit is love, joy, peace, forbearance, kindness, goodness faithfulness, gentleness and self-control. Against such things there is no law."

—Galatians 5:22 (NIV)

"For now we see only a reflection as in a mirror then we shall see face to face. Now I know in part. Then I shall know fully even as I am fully known. And now the three remain: faith hope and love. But the greatest of these is love."

—1 Corinthians 13:12-13 (NIV)

"Now may God, the fountain of hope, fill you to overflowing with uncontainable joy and perfect peace as you trust in him. And may the power of the Holy Spirit continually surround your life with his super-abundance until you radiate with hope!"

—Romans 15:13 (TPT)

Worship becomes a weapon. Let the high praises of God always be in your mouth. It becomes a two-edged sword in your hand. (**Psalm 149:6**) The Lord is always watching over you to keep you from harm. Having a Spiritual Altar provides a place for you to hear from the Lord. (Genesis 12:8) Imagine one word from the Lord would rechart your course for life. One Angelic Appearance will redirect your steps. Commit now to seek and to "feel" His joy and to *"know"* in your heart He Loves you. Time at your Spiritual Altar deepens your intimacy with the Lord. Abraham honored God with His Spiritual Altar at Bethel. It will nourish your soul both naturally and spiritually. The loving presence of Jesus heals like a balm like no other. His Precious Love locks into the memory cells of your heart. It will clear your heart of old and outdated beliefs. It will refresh your resolve to stand and stay strong with the Lord through praise and worship! It will cause you to say NO to man and Yes to the Lord more and more, and you will release no guilt in saying NO. Slowly you are being conformed to the image he desires for you. I once saw a video by Dr. Mike Evans entitled *Walking in the Favor of God*, calling us to radically embrace *obedience, humility, forgiveness, and generosity*, which he believes formulates God's Spiritual DNA. God's

DNA reveals His Mandate for us. The more we seek His Kingdom, the Lord gives us circumstances to help us deepen these mandates. They come not to bring trouble. They become a blessing through the lessons learned as we endure and persevere through them.

"Consider it pure joy my brothers and sisters, whenever you face trials of many kinds, because you know that the testing of your faith produces perseverance."

—James 1:2-5 (NIV)

Perseverance opens the door of boldness. In a little while, these qualities will automatically manifest in your being. It shows up in the way you speak and the words you use. You find yourself renewed in your mind by hearing with a new, unshakable ear. (**Romans 12:2**) A Godly tenderness comes upon you. Your refined actions show love to your beloved partner and your family. My guess, they can see something new changing in you as your heart becomes hungry for the Lord. Yes, you must seek the Lord to turn on the Holy Spirit faucet of this outpouring of the Spirit into your vessel. Seek the Holy Spirit to deepen your wisdom and revelation to know him more deeply. Seek your heart to be enlightened to see what Yeshua sees for you. Well, let's be clear about this. He sees it because He placed His Desires within you. You are His Vessel. (**2 Corinthians 4:7**). Your destiny matters because it releases a sweetness of the Presence delivered to your soul. He helps you become unshakable. It matters to gift the kingdom with your talents. He opens doors and windows no one can shut. One time I flew into Salina, Kansas to visit my parents in Holyrood, a couple of hours south. Dad and Mom picked me and only Dad came to drive me back when I was ready to fly back home. I drove and we talked. Sure enough, I said goodbye, got on the plane and there was Dad on the tarmac waving...Keys! Oh dear, I had the keys. So, I had the stewardess to give them to the pilot to open his window and threw them out! Unshakable.

The Key to being unshakable is to *become quiet in your soul* to fix your eyes on Him and talk to Him with all you think, say, and do. It is waiting on the Lord for Him to direct our steps and our path to mold us. He gives us the Keys to the Kingdom opening doors no man can shut! (**Isaiah 22:22**) He is the potter, and we become His clay creation. (**Isaiah 68:4**) He wants to pour the Spirit into you to bless your life. Then, Christ lives in you. Having intimacy with the Beloved Christ will shift your beloved's knowing you more intimately. Intimacy with the Lord must first begin with you for your resistance to be released. Suddenly, when this happens you become *unshakable in your knowing.* His joy will seep into every place you walk and with whom to talk. Then the wisdom and revelation begin to appear. You will be an overcomer breaking through anything in the way of your walk with the Lord. Guard your joy. Keep asking for Love and Self Control, the bookends of the Fruits, to be revealed. Understand the Fruits of the Spirit (**Galatians 5:22**) to deepen your intimacy with Jesus and your partner, your lover. It will heal a heavy heart. *It will ignite joy today!!!*

"Yet you, Lord are our Father. We are the clay you are the potter; we are all the work of your hands."

—Isaiah 64:8 (NIV)

"So above all, constantly seek God's kingdom and his righteousness then all these less important things will be given to you abundantly. Refuse to worry about tomorrow, but deal with each challenge that comes your way, one day at a time. Tomorrow will take care of itself."

—Matthew 6:33-34 (TPT)

"I keep asking that the God of our Lord Jesus Christ, the glorious Father, may give you the Spirit of wisdom and revelation, so that you may know him better. I pray that the eyes of our heart may be enlightened in order that you may know the hope to which he has called you, the riches of his glorious inheritance and in his holy people, and his incomparably great power for us who believe."

—Ephesians 1: 17-19 (NIV)

His "Love Softened My Heart." My breakthrough came calling with Empower 2000 and Dr. Joseph Peck's Kingdom-Based Webinar Company, answering my prayers. I pulled away from a life in the New Age Church to fully embrace the Lord Jesus through these webinars. They created such a hunger and thirst in me for the Lord. It gave me the answer to my *"Burning Bushes,"* often appearing in my meditations!!! They were burning alive with the Lord's desire. Can you imagine attending church all my life and not knowing the *Burning Bush* called Moses to serve the Father God. (**Exodus 3:2**) I realized I always knew about Jesus, yet I did not know Him as my Lord. As I fell in Love with Jesus, my life shifted to embrace the Holy Spirit. Jesus poured His Living Water into my soul. My heart opened to receive him. I was so parched and dry. The door opened to let my heart receive the Love Jesus has for me. His Love for me softened my heart. I found others who were walking with the Lord's Love, on fire for the Lord!!! I discovered what it meant to be with the Lord's "Hot Coals!" How about you? Are you parched as well? Do you know the Father, the Son, and the Holy Spirit? Do you truly know how much you are loved?

"I love each of you with the same love that the Father loves me. You must continually let my love nourish your hearts."

—John 15:9 (TPT) *As a little girl I recall my bedroom walls were filled with roses. One at eye level was my focus. I feel the Lord Love came to me through that rose.*

"Love never stops loving. It extends beyond the gift of prophecy, which eventually fades away. It is more enduring than tongues, which will one day fall silent. Love remains long after words of knowledge are forgotten."

—1 Corinthians 13:8-9 (TPT)

"Let the inner movement of your heart always be to love one another and never pay the role of an actor wearing a mask. Despise evil and embrace everything that is good and virtuous."

—Romans 12:9 (TPT)

"Dear friends let us love one another for love comes from God. Everyone who loves has been born of God and knows God. Whoever does not love does not know God because God is love."

—1 John 4:7 (NIV)

"And to we know and rely on the love God has for us. God is love Whoever lives in love lives in God, and God in them."

—1 John 4:16 (NIV)

God's Love helped me release fears. *Fears were released about my partner as a knowing trust arose. Clearly, this was my weakness where only Yeshua could provide me strength.* (**2 Corinthians 12:9-10**) The Living Word moved me into the world of the Holy Spirit with bread and meat to satisfy. Yeshua/Jesus, the Living Word, helped move me away from New Age reasoning. *Jesus is the Way, the Truth, and the Life, and only through Him can one go to the Father.* The Holy Spirit began showing me many areas of my life to seek forgiveness. I repented to take responsibility for the ways I had stepped away from the Lord. There is no fear in God's perfect Love because fear has to do with punishment. The one who fears is not perfect in Love. This opens the way to Love God and Love God's People placing and your trust in Him (**Psalm 37:3**) to love God with all your heart, soul, and mind. (**Mark 12:30-31**) With God's Love I began to understand repentance for the first time in nearly 75 years. I can remember singing *Amazing Grace* and not saying the word *wretch like me* because it didn't apply. How shallow and prideful to think this way. I believe Fear of the Lord and His Glory released will cause many to come to the Body of Christ. The remnant groans for revival, yet the church remains passive and lukewarm, being satisfied with milk. The Lord has the boldness of the older generation engaged.

The Lord is using my generation to step boldly into His Purpose and Calling. Well into their wisdom years, the women of the Boomer Generation are here to serve His Purpose to equip and help train Baby Believers just baptized. Even as I write, this shift is happening. Now, I see the preparation for the Lord was getting me ready for such a time as this. If my writing can save even one soul to the Kingdom, then it will be a success! Those who seek Jesus will never be forsaken. (**Joshua 1:5**) Jesus is the same yesterday, today, and forever. Jesus has assured me the healing of my family's salvation will be His to do mine is to Love. Love heals and delivers. His Holy Spirit makes clear the way. Our job, yours, and mine, calls for us to Know Him and *become His Love.*

"I am the way and the truth and the life. No one comes to the father except through me."

—John 14:6 (NIV)

"Jesus Christ is the same yesterday and today and forever."

—Hebrews 13:8 (NIV)

HOW THE HOLY SPIRIT BECAME MY DEFAULT SERVER

The door to the occult opened in High School using the Ouija board with my girlfriends. In came the enemy. Suddenly friends showed up interested in the occult. Then, at 25, the study of reincarnation followed by an intense interest in *astrology and horoscopes.* (**Isaiah 47:13**) Clearly, I did not and could not have known the outcome of these decisions. Given an inch, the enemy will turn it into a mile. No wonder I would feel so comfortable all those years with the New Age Message. Holy Spirit conviction called me to repentance. Through reading the bible, I found my solution. Jesus. With a great deal of repentance, I began to seek forgiveness. Holy Spirit revealed exactly what would shift me back on the path to the Lord Jesus. When you are clear about Knowing Jesus, then your faith becomes crystal clear. Like a line drawn in the sand, *no going back.* Instead, the Living Word filled my thirst to discover a Well-Watered Garden of the Lord. (**Isaiah 58:11**) It revealed the only blueprint to be followed removing any personal agenda to embrace God's Purpose and Calling on my life. That meant there was a calling on my partner's life as well. Only Jesus can make this happen.

"Now, it is God himself who has anointed us. And he constantly is strengthening both you and us in union with Christ. He knows we are his since he has also stamped his seal of love over our hearts and has given us the Holy Spirit like an engagement ring is given to a bride—down payment of the blessings to come!"

—**2 Corinthians 1:21-22** (TPT)

Continue to press toward for the Holy Spirit to awaken your partner. We cannot talk enough about the need to immerse ourselves in the Holy Spirit who brings refreshing clarity from Jesus. The Lord is the Vine, and I am His branch. (**John 15:1-4**) As I remain in Him and He in me I will bear much fruit. The Vine does all the work being rooted to supply me all that I need to flourish. Water, nutrients, and vital sap flows to me naturally. The Holy Spirit delivers them. I simply await and receive them. Of myself I am nothing. Deny yourself to take up the Lord's Cross for Victory! (**Matthew 16:24**) Go forth and sin no more! (**Romans 6:6**) Therefore, I must depend completely and totally on the Lord Jesus, my Vine. Andrew Murray in *Humility and Absolute Surrender* tells us the Vine has total responsibility. We are to rest in Him to receive and bear fruit. (**John 15:8**) I must keep my branch free from grieving the Holy Spirit with foul language, bitterness, or anxiety to produce fruit. When we learn to depend completely on God, then everything turns out just right. (**Proverbs 3:5-6**) This puts our trust in the Lord above all our own understanding. Clarity begins to emerge with the Holy Spirit Presence. Consider Benny Hinn's book, *Good Morning Holy Spirit* for clarity to immense yourself in the Spirit.

Clarity in Christ ushers in new discernment from the Holy Spirit, the First Person of the Godhead. Through the awesome Power of the Holy Spirit, you will move mountains. I always wondered why Jesus was never quoted in New Age messages and articles. The only way to know anything calls for the Living Word to verify and witness. This becomes a way to make the Path of the Lord our only path. Just saying His Name gives you power. To be the Living Image of Christ, He mandates us to obey His commands with humility with reverence with repentance to turn away and return. Salvation is found in no one else. Give glory to the Power of Jesus' Name.

"But you will receive power when the Holy spirit comes on you; and you will be my witnesses in Jerusalem, and in all Judea and Samaria, and to the ends of the earth."

—**Acts 1:8** Jesus instructs the disciples before ascending.

"Salvation is found in no one else, for there is no other name under heaven given to mankind by which we must be saved."

—**Acts 4:12** (NIV)

"The Son is the radiance of God's glory and the exact representation of his being, sustaining all things by his powerful word."

—**Hebrews 1:2** (NIV)

Repercussion comes after Repentance in my dictionary!!! That says it all! It sheds new light on why feeling remorse is needed daily to own up to mistakes, not just Sundays. Practicing righteousness will ease the pain and clear the way to prevent repercussions! (**Mark 1:15**) Why is it so hard to say I am so sorry; will you forgive me? It became a new lens of understanding to view unbelief in myself! How about my wrong-doing or my judgment of others? My Spirit was leading me to consider my partner with ownership of the part I play. Maybe it is more about me than him, I began to question. At the same time, my lack of humility was revealed in how I handled issues at home. Dr. Joseph Peck often taught repentance found in the **2 Chronicles 7:14** passage, telling us that God will do three things if we do four things. In all my places of worship I have attended until now, I cannot recall a single mention of Repentance. Many churches do not even acknowledge the Holy Spirit much less repentance. (**Revelation 3:15-16**) Repentance requires humility to humble yourself to confess. This calls for surrender to the Will of the Father. The Holy Spirit made me look at *my own humility*. I called upon the Lord many times over many situations that seemed to repeat themselves revealing the patterns of behavior. These played themselves out in anger and words of regret with my husband. My heavy heart began to lift with the idea I *needed the changing, not him*! Humble yourself and pray. Seek His Face and turn from wicked ways. Well, the turn part began to become apparent. Humility brings such gifts of understanding. The Father's Love awakens us to know more deeply humility helps us grow spiritually for our partners.

"If my people, who are called by my name, will humble themselves and pray and seek my face and turn from their wicked ways then I will hear from heaven and I will forgive their sin and will heal their land."

—**2 Chronicles 7:14** (NIV)

God assigns us to sift and shift our spiritual growth. Never did I imagine presenting webinars on the DNA of God! This assignment came out of the blue! I helped to create a weekly series as a follow-up to Dr. Peck's 40 Days of Prayer Revolution. Every Thursday these webinars were offered from January to August 2019 with a break in May. Finally, Dr. Peck asked us to present a class series entitled *Attracting the Favor of God.* We worked together on this assignment from God. It covered God's Radical DNA Mandates: *Obedience, Humility, Forgiveness, and Generosity*, a concept from Dr. Mike Evans, who has stood in defense of Israel for the past fifty years. In his video, *Walking in the Favor of God*, our eyes were opened to the Master Plan of spiritual living. Repentance comes from radical Obedience to God. Yeshua only did as His Father instructed him. His Spirit guides us to obey. Yes, follow the Spirit to embrace your awareness and sensitivity. Your actions reflect a new language, new thoughts, patience, kindness, releasing old patterns, and much more. It is all a part of Putting on Christ. My prayer life blossomed with an established Sacred Time. I began to see my life from a whole new and higher perspective. My husband began to feel the change of my love with Jesus shining through me. Finally, I was learning to *put on Christ.*

"Love is patient, love is kind. It does not envy, it does not boast., it is not proud. It does not dishonor others. It is not self-seeking, it is not easily angered, it keeps no record of wrongs. Love does not delight in evil but rejoices with the truth. It always protects, always trust, always hopes, always perseveres."

—1 Corinthians 13:4-6 (NIV)

JESUS CHRIST IS MUCH MORE THAN MY FRIEND.

All my life, I loved the 23rd Psalm. The Lord is my Shepherd. Even in the New Age moments, my Shepherd still regarded me as His Sheep. Jesus, my friend, was now my Shepherd guiding me the Power of His Name. The Names of the Father are so very holy. A recent Bible Study on the Names of God was stunning to me open a new world of comfort through understanding the nature of the Father's names. (**Psalm 9:10**) *"Those who know your name Lord, trust you, and you, Lord, have never forsaken those who seek you."* Because of this verse, I began to learn the names of God. Worship took on a new meaning for me with this new awareness.

These names are His many promises. There is power in the Name of Jesus. (**2 Timothy 1:7**) *The Names of God move us to fellowship with a deeper trust to be transformed, renewed, rescued, and delivered.* God's Word is a blueprint, a Living Word, a Living roadmap, and a Living Sword as well. Jesus is the Living Word made flesh. Daily I call upon the Names of the Lord. There is tremendous power in just saying the Names of Jesus. His Name offers protection. His Name will deliver you from the enemy. Call on Yeshua often. *"Help me, Yeshua!" "Help me, Jesus!" "Jesus! Jesus! Jesus!"*

"Yahweh is my best friend and my shepherd. I always have more than enough. He offers a resting place for me in his luxurious love. His tracks take me to an oasis of peace near the quiet brook of bliss!"

—Psalm 23:1-2 (TPT)

"I am the good shepherd. The good shepherd lays down his life for the sheep."

—John 10:11 (NIV)

Exalting the Holy Names of the Father T.H.G.A.T.G. which means *To Him Give All the Glory.* The Holy Spirit leads me to give praise to the titles and attributes of Our Father's Name. Yeshua truly unfolded more deeply as my Shepherd, Jehovah Rohi. My Sheep, hear my voice. I love Yehovah Magen: I Am Your Shield. Jehovah Kabodi: I Am The Glorious One. Jehovah Shalom: I Am Your Peace. Shalom asks the question, are you whole with peace. Truly this one is visual, Yehovah Tsur: I Am Your Rock. Yehovah Chereb: I Am the Glorious Sword. **Psalm 91** speaks of Yehovah Ma'ozi: I Am Your Fortress. Yehovah Anokhi: I Am Your Purpose. Our Father, we bless you Yehovah Nissi: I Am your Banner. Finally, Yehovah Jireh: The Lord Will Provide. (**Genesis 22:13**) The Ram is in the Bush. Place yourself visually with these powerful images. Consider your own name. Dr. Myles in *The Order of Melchizedek* tells us in the ancient world of the Jewish people, names embraced a prophetic calling, a spiritual destiny and became "signposts" of their character. Abraham became the Father of the Nations with his name change. The Father's many attributes are revealed through His Titles. T.H.G.A.T.G. *To Him Give All The Glory*

Again, consider the "signposts" of your name for your spiritual destiny.

"Glory to God in the highest heaven, and on earth peace to those on whom his favor rests."

—Luke 2:14 (NIV)

"Let them praise your great and awesome name—he is holy."

—Psalms 99:3 (NIV)

"Let everyone praise this breathtaking God, for he is holy."

—Psalms 99:3 (TPT)

Astonishing Joy comes when you are ready to follow the Lord's teachings commandments. You belong to Him and return to Him to be refreshed and renewed with a new life. Call to Him. Yes, the Lord will provide and, we need to follow what He commands us to do. The Lord loves us just as the Father loved Him. The more we embrace this, the Lord will provide a blessing in our marriage unions. Knowing God is with me every step of the way becomes my strength to persevere. **(James 1:2-3)** Be encouraged to seek Your Lord calling for His Names. He meets all our needs. Even for those who live in unbelief, He

Provides. (**Mark 9:24**) Because I know the Lord will never forsake me, I embrace relationships with an expectation of a healing miracle for them, especially my family. I know I am not alone in this conflict of unbelief. Stepping away from pleasing the world to please the Father God naturally follows your obedience. It causes my discernment of the world to deepen. I expect wisdom with these miracles, and I expect to become a miracle not just for my husband and for my whole family. Set aside time to Wait on the Lord for your next steps.

Time spent *Waiting on the Lord* helped me to increase my *faith and trust in my Heavenly Father*. Without agenda, set aside time to worship, wait, and exalt the Lord. Finally, embrace the revelation from resting in Him for His transformation and renewal. I so love and daily decree (**Ephesians 1:17-19**) directing me to seek greater wisdom and revelation. This results in a change of the mind that leads to a change of the heart which leads to a change in actions which comes through prayer.

"I keep asking that the God of our Lord Jesus Christ, the glorious Father, may give you the Spirit of Wisdom and Revelation so that you may know Him better. I pray that the eyes of your heart may be enlightened in order that you may know the hope to which he has called you, the riches of his glorious inheritance in his holy people, and his incomparably great power for us who believe."

—Ephesians 1:17-19 (NIV)

"Do not be conformed to this world but be transformed by the renewing of your mind. That you may prove what is that good and acceptable and perfect will of God."

—Romans 12:2 (NIV)

"Those who know your name trust in you. For you, Lord, have never forsaken those who seek you."

—Psalm 9:10 (NIV)

"We need to know Him to obey Him."

—John 8:49 (NIV)

"My sheep listen to my voice; I know them and they follow me. I give them eternal life and they shall never perish no one will snatch them out of my hand."

—John 10:27-28 (NIV)

"The Lord watches over you—the Lord is your right hand; the sun will not harm you day by day nor the moon at night."

—Psalm 121:4-5 (NIV)

"And my God will meet all your needs according to the riches of his glory in Christ Jesus."

—Philippians 4:19 (NIV)

"Whoever says, "I know Him," but does not do what he commands is a liar, and the truth is not in that person."

—1 John 2:4 (NIV)

"Love the Lord your God with all your heart and with all your soul and with all your mind."

—**Matthew 22:37** (NIV) *This is our first and greatest commandment.*

Pray and Praise to God for all comfort through prayer. Prayers to the Father become a pathway to the Throne of Grace. How we pray will make all the difference. All scriptures are God Breathed. (**2 Timothy 3:16**) Therefore, they are living scriptures to be used for teaching, rebuking, correcting, and training in righteousness. Through Yeshua, God has given all authority on heaven and earth. God will always say Yes and Amen to His Son's desires. Prophet Robin Bullock shared on Elijah's Streaming with Steve Schultz regarding prayers directed to the Father God in Jesus Name will always be a Yes and Amen. (**2 Corinthians 1:20**) *When praying for the salvation of a beloved he taught to pray to the Father in Jesus Name for the perfect laborer to be sent to their beloved. Every person will listen to someone. Thus, prayers to the Father based on a promise of the scriptures in the Name of Jesus will always be a Yes and Amen to the Lord Jesus who has dominion over the earth.* It is approaching the Father in the Name of the Son with scriptures (**Acts 1:14**, *the disciples One Accord Prayer*, **Isaiah 53:4-5, 1 Peter 2:24, Psalm 107:20**) *This is so comforting.* Faith is at the foundation of this principle. All prayer is based on your Faith in the promises of the Father's Word. Whatever your request, such as a need to be met, the *perfect laborer to be sent* or a healing to manifest will be done through the Name of Jesus. **1 Peter 2:24** is a great scripture for being healed by Jesus' Wounds. Please turn to the Holiness of the Father to direct your prayers for healings of every kind. Expect an answer, then watch and wait to see God's activity for you. May our prayers reach the bowls of heaven to be poured back down upon us.

"No matter how many promises God has made, they are "Yes" in Christ. And so through him the "Amen" is spoken by us to the glory of God."

—2 Corinthians 1:20 (NIV)

"You did not choose me, but I chose you and appointed you so that you might go and bear fruit—fruit that will last—and so that whatever you ask in my name the Father will give you."

—John 15:16 (NIV)

"All scripture is God-breathed and is useful for teaching, rebuking, correcting, and training in righteousness so that the servant of God (that is us in prayer) may be thoroughly equipped for every good work."

—2 Timothy 3:16-17 (NIV)

"He himself bore our sins" in his body on the cross, so that we might die to sins and live for righteousness; "by his wounds you have been healed."

—2 Peter 2:24 (NIV)

"...and provide for those who grieve in Zion—to bestow on them a crown of beauty instead of ashes, the oil of Joy instead of mourning, and a garment of praise instead of a spirit of despair. They will be called oaks of righteousness, a planting of the Lord for the display of his splendor."

—Isaiah 61:3 (NIV)

God's revelation began moving in My life and through my prayers.
His plans for me were being revealed while resting and waiting on Him.

Through quiet reflection, I viewed my life, and it also helped me understand the life of my partner from a much higher perspective. **It helped me see Jesus lives in my partner as well. This was a new way for me to tenderly embrace my beloved partner, just as the Lord watches over us. I began Waiting on the Lord, My First Love, who was showing me the way, step by step, how to use His Love through me.** Thus, I began waiting on my partner. Soon I heard from the Holy Spirit more and more. Daily, hidden things were revealed. My steps began to be ordered. I spent more time with him. I was gaining trust and confidence with my partner. More and more, I felt the Presence of Christ backed by the Power of the Name of the Lord Jesus. When we are in Him, His Power gives us the strength we need to persevere. We persevere because we Know Him.

"For it is with your heart that you believe and are justified and it is with your mouth that you profess your faith and are saved."

—Romans 10:10 (NIV)

TIME TO REVIEW AND JOURNAL YOUR REFECTIONS.

Do this before moving to the second petition.

- Do you have a relationship with the Holy Spirit in your life? Do you talk with him?

- Do you have a Sacred Time established devoted to the Lord? A Sacred Altar Place in a private place to honor the Lord?

- Do you begin your prayer time with praise and thanksgiving?

- Do you sense in your heart when the Holy Spirit's conviction happens? Obey with repentance?

- Do you seek revelation by waiting on the Lord to know your next move with your spouse?

- Have you been Born from Above by the Holy Spirit? Do you speak in God's Language of Tongues?

DECLARATION: Today, I seek the Holy Spirit to show the way to know the Lord more deeply to enlighten my heart.

REFLECT ON THE FOLLOWING AND WRITE YOUR THOUGHTS IN YOUR PRAYER JOURNAL:

- YOUR THOUGHTS TO JESUS

- IDEAS AND WORDS FROM JESUS

- YOUR THOUGHTS

Spend time to express in writing ways repentance has brought you to know the Lord. **(2 Corinthians 7:10**) Does reconciliation of your feelings about your spouse come to you? Are you able to see your partner from a higher perspective? *What is one thing you can do tonight before going to bed to find joy?*

PRAYER: *Heavenly and Beloved Father, I come to give you all praise and thanksgiving for clearing my path and showing me the way, Lord, to help me to know you more deeply by the renewal of my mind. I offer you my heart to profess your glory over my marriage and my life. I receive your light to overcome the dark places in my life. Examine my heart Lord to clear away that which is out of alignment with you. Align me, Lord, with your plans and purposes. Receive my repentance Lord with forgiveness and cleansing. Precious Lord, help me radiate your Love for my partner's salvation to see and feel you and to know you, Lord. Come Holy Spirit, you are welcome here. Whisper to me the way to go. Be my comforter this day. In Jesus Precious Name, Amen*

Chapter 2
STEWARDSHIP

Thy Kingdom Come

SIFT AND SHIFT YOUR UNION WITH OBEDIENCE—KNOWING THE WAY TO GO AND WALK IN IT

CHEF NOTE: Sometimes, it takes great patience to understand a new recipe. Especially one with complex instructions. When I obey the instructions, I am usually on track for success at the table. If, on the other hand, I decided to add the baking powder at the wrong time or skip a step entirely, well, it just might not rise as expected. As a newly married, I remember hilarious moments in the kitchen! One time I used the entire garlic head instead of just one clove in a new recipe. Who knew! Well, after that, I did! How about the time I took frozen bread to a spaghetti dinner party, not realizing the directions were on the bottom of the bread. During a lively dinner, what a riot to discover we were eating the instructions! *Wow!* As a more seasoned kitchener, I recall another example of waste not want not moment with a family favorite called Taco Chicken. Absolutely a winner! Be sure to check it out in the recipes section, along with several other tried and tested family favorites! Having not used all the taco seasoning mixture, I decided to add to the recipe anyway. Honestly, I remember a still small voice telling me to be careful. It ruined the whole dish. I did not obey the instructions, such as remove the label for baking!!!!

You know the Lord mandates that we use that same approach to obedience with Him. Obey His Commands. His Instructions. Obedience is honoring God. Listen and obey the still small voice. Jesus only spoke what the Father wanted Him to reveal. He obeyed the Father to bring salvation to all humanity. Following Jesus' Commands will change your world. The greater your compliance, the greater the blessings from Him. Unheard of Blessings, Divine Blessings when you submit to Him.

Lord, I pray thy Kingdom will come through me, Lord, walking in the Spirit. Prayer and meditation opened the door to understand that obedience to the Lord *creates the way* for our anointing to serve in the Body of Christ in a more meaningful way. Obedience calls for acts of applying and obeying. When we seek the Kingdom to come through us, we must put aside and deny ourselves, our understandings, and opinions. This calls for you to *submit and commit* yourself to the Lord, to His Will and worship Him in the Spirit. **(Deuteronomy 28)**

"God is spirit, and his worshipers must worship in the Spirit and in truth."

—**John 4:24** (NIV)

We worship Jesus in the Spirit seeking new life and His Living Waters. **(John 4:13-14)** His offer of Living Water leads us to a new Eternal Life in Christ with a deeper awareness of the Father. We can all learn from the Samaritan Woman at the well recognizing and knowing Jesus as Messiah. Her belief brought the entire town to Him. She believed and made herself available. We must make ourselves both available and willing to step in to be a servant for the Lord. This includes worship. God seeks those who worship Him, knowing Him in Spirit and truth, not with rituals and absent hearts. Christ will speak to you just like He did the Samaritan woman. Surrender yourself for the Father through the Holy Spirit. (**Psalm 37:7**) Because He directs the Father's Will, you need Him to direct your will as well. Submitting self opens the door for renewal of the mind by the Holy Spirit to show you not only to follow Jesus but to obey His Word.

"Everyone who drinks this water will be thirsty again, but whoever drinks the water I give them will never thirst. Indeed, the water I give them will become in them a spring of water welling up to eternal life."

—John 4:13-14 (NIV)

"Submit yourselves the to God. Resist the devil and he will flee from you."

—James 4:7 (NIV)

Say out loud now…in fact, get on your knees with me and repet this prayer:

*"Oh Lord, I need your help! Help me understand your ways, Lord. Give me an understanding heart so I can passionately know and obey your truth for my life. Reveal to me, Father, any former thinking not alignment with you, Lord. Release, remove and forever shift my mind to embrace your stability Lord, as in (**Isaiah 33:6**), your foundation for my times. Place before me, Lord, words to change my life. Decree over me, Lord necessary change. Lord, renew me to only know your will and way and not conform to the world. On my knees, Lord, I repent for my*

ways and desire but one thing, Lord, for your Kingdom to come and Your Will be done through me Lord just as it is in Heaven. In Jesus' Mighty Name, Amen."

"He will be the sure foundation of your times, a rich store of salvation and wisdom and knowledge; the fear of the Lord is key to this treasure."

—Isaiah 33:6 (NIV)

LISTEN. TRUST. OBEY—SUBMIT TO THE LORD

Discipline deepens your Spiritual Maturity. I love the song *Trust and Obey,* because there is no other way to find happiness in Jesus unless we *trust and obey.* (**Psalm 28:7**) Only when I am in Him with obedience will I find joy. We must submit our personal agenda to become His Vessel to fill. This may be the time the Lord reveals those things of a carnal nature which keeps us focused on the flesh fighting with God's Plans and probably, at some point, refusing to obey His Direction. (**Romans 8:7-8**) V8 Goes on to say no matter how hard we try; God still finds no pleasure with the person controlled by the flesh. This speaks of following the crowd or going along with something knowing it is wrong. Gossip, for example. This is a needed transformation coming from the Love of the Father to spiritually draw a line in the sand. When it begins to flow through you, the cleansing begins. We seek a new identity in Christ seated in heavenly places. Submitting to obedience awakens who you are. Sometimes discipline from the Lord reveals the necessity to submit through repeating experiences until understanding comes. (**Proverbs 3:5-6**) Discipline brings relief. All of this comes when we surrender our hearts to the Lord.

Surrender to the Lord, we Submit to His Holy Spirit. Loren Helms speaks of submitting to the Lord in his book, *The Voice in the Wilderness.* (**Matthew 3:3**) Obedience stops the urges of self-assertion. "If only we would be willing to consistently wait with joy upon God, He will refine us. There are fires to pass through as we wait, which will burn out the dross and leave pure gold. So, self-assertion comes when we *stop* praying and *stop* listening for the voice of God." Self-assertion stops the Holy Spirit Presence from working through us. Finally, Loren says, *"We cannot take one step after Jesus unless we deny self and listen for God's guidance."* This prepares a pathway for shifting the way you think, what you say and how you say it. Submitting shifts your life. Being disciplined leads to obedience. Obedience leads to gifts of fresh mercy.

My Natural Father gifted me years ago with a can of wheat from our farm in Downs, Kansas. You remember the old Folger's Coffee Cans that were tin? From one of our harvests, Dad filled up the can with wheat and gave it to me as a gift. That was over 40 years ago. Since that time, I have moved the can of wheat from freezer to freezer for all these years. During one of our Empower 2000 webinars the subject of dying to oneself like wheat was discussed. In the dark earth the seed dies, then cracks open to spout and grows with nurturing rains to multiply a hundredfold. I told the story of my Folger's can of wheat from our family farm in Kansas. Dr. Peck offered that this can of wheat could feed a nation. (**John 3:30**) We too, must die to ourselves for the Lord to produce a hundredfold crop of blessings through us. Our surrender opens the door for us to serve and worship Jesus.

"I have been crucified with Christ and I no longer live but Christ lives in me. The life I now live in the body, I live by faith in the Son of God who loved me and gave himself for me."

—Galatians 2:20 (NIV)

"Endure hardship as discipline; God is treating you as his children. For what children are not disciplined by their father? If you are not disciplined—and everyone undergoes discipline—then you are not legitimate, not true sons and daughters at all."

—Hebrews 12:7-8 (NIV)

Open the door of your heart with a worship song! I love the song: *Have Thine Own Way, Lord* to mold and me after your will Lord. Do this while I am yielded and still in my daily devotions. I sing to the Lord as a part of my devotional worship. (**Jeremiah 20:13**) Growing up with hymns, I find they have great messages in them, so I ordered a Methodist Hymnal from Amazon! With my favorite hymns marked, I sing during my worship time every morning. My heart knows these hymns. I sing to the Lord throughout the day and, He sings over me. Imagine the Lord singing over us with our own special song. What would yours be?

I begin my Sacred Time with Shirley Goodness. I open my prayer time singing the 23rd Psalm to my own tune ending with goodness and mercy. I love the story about the little boy who tells a friend someone called Shirley Goodness follows me every day of my life. May your personal Angel Goodness and Angel Mercy follow you all the days of your life as well!!! Make Shirley Goodness your best friend! (**Psalm 23:6**) Decide today to sing your Psalms!!! Put your name in all the scriptures to personalize them to speak to your soul. Ask the Lord before going to bed to give you a scripture for the next day. Imagine the Angels in heaven singing to the Father with the sound of their wings and continuous song. Sort of reminds me of the 4th verse of Amazing Grace with *no less days to sing His Praise than when we first begun!*

"…speaking to one another with psalms, hymns, and songs from the Spirit. Sing and make music from your heart to the Lord always giving thanks to God, the Father, for everything, in the name of our Lord Jesus Christ."

—Ephesians 5:19-20 (NIV)

The work of a perfumer. Sweeter. During the singing of the 23rd Psalm, when preparing a table before my enemy, I anoint myself with Sacred Oils. Sandie Freed used these anointings for her well-received online Empower 2000 class "Dethroning Jezebel (Part 2)—Breaking the Demonic Threefold Cord of Jezebel Athaliah, and Delilah." She tells us anointing oils prepare us to be the Bride of the King. They prepare us to walk in the fullness of our spiritual authority. **Psalm 23:5** *"You prepare a table before me in the presence of my enemies, You, anoint my head with oil; my cup overflows."* I prepare myself daily to be the Bride anointed in the fullness of obedience to Yeshua with:

The oil of Frankincense—extracted from a tree, pierced for sap to run. It means "white." *Death to myself, dying to my agenda for Lord's Will; the Blood of the Lamb makes me white as snow* (**Isaiah 1:18**)

Calamus—grows tall and reedy-like amid clay—*a strength of character, Holy Character*

Cinnamon—comes from the bark *of* a tree with *sweetness*. It means *"to stand upright, to walk in the righteousness of the Lord."* Knowing right from wrong

The Esther Anointing of Myrrh—granted Esther with *spiritual authority*. It is known as a bitter from the root word for myrrh being

Marah. It means—*enduring the bitterness.* Each of us must endure the myrrh anointing, *turning any bitterness into an Oil of Joy.*

When I bless myself with cinnamon, I always think about my Aunt Becky, who called me *"Sweeter!"* Little did I know she was anointing me with the **23rd Psalm.** These oils come together to becomes an **Oil of Joy,** which anoints and protects me for the day ahead. Holy Spirit confers to me the strength that comes from an oil anointing. (**James 5:14**) A most remarkable gift of oils arrived one day out of the blue. Calamus, Cinnamon, and Myrrh. The mystery gift was solved when I met with my Australian Prayer partner, Tracey James. *She gifted me so perfectly from the below scripture. She has gone on to develop* soaps from these oils from Piping Rock. She embraces the anointing as the Lord's Perfumer.

Then the Lord said to Moses, "Take the following fine spices: 500 shekels of liquid myrrh, half as much of fragrant cinnamon 250 shekels of fragrant calamus, 500 shekels of cassia—all according to the sanctuary shekel and a hin of olive oil. Make thee into a sacred anointing oil, a fragrant blend the works of a perfumer. It will be the sacred anointing oil. V 34 Take fragrant spices—gum, resin onycha and galbanum and pure frankincense, all in equal amounts, and make a fragrant blend of incense the work of a perfumer. It is to be salted and pure and sacred."

—Exodus 30:22-25, 34 (NIV)

"The Lord has anointed me to proclaim good news to the poor.....to proclaim the year of the Lord's favor and the day of vengeance of our God to comfort all who mourn and provide for those who grieve in Zion, to bestow on them a crown of beauty instead of ashes, the oil of joy instead of mourning and a garment of praise instead of a spirit of despair."

—Isaiah 61:3 (NIV)

"Your plants are an orchard of pomegranates with choice fruits, with henna and nard, and saffron, calamus and cinnamon with every kind of incense tree, with myrrh and aloes and all the finest species."

—Song of Songs 4:13 (NIV)

Obedience anoints us with confidence *to receive Authority and Position of Power.* It means dying to myself to step into the destiny the Lord has planned for me. For me to know my future, I must listen for God to speak to me. I must put my time in His Hands. (**Psalm 31:14-15**) An audible word from Yeshua would totally shift your life forever. A still small voice of Holy Spirit guidance, though quiet, will do the same. When these thoughts come, obey them. If you don't, then later, as you become more awakened, you will see the results of not heeding them. If ever Holy Spirit reminds you of an item to buy at the store, do it because you will need it! *Just do it!* I recall shopping during a recent hurricane this past summer where the stores in Florida were literally emptied out. Late getting there, I declared to the Lord, I would find everything on my list. (**2 Corinthians 9:8**) Guess what? It was so delightful to see one left of what I needed tucked away for me. It calls us to prepare enough for God to multiply and provide. Do not worry about not having enough. This thought brings me such comfort.

"And my God will meet all your needs according to the riches of his glory in Christ Jesus."

—Philippians 4:19 (NIV)

"Now he who supplies seed to the sower and bread for food will also supply and increase your store of seed and will enlarge the harvest of your righteousness."

—2 Corinthians 9:10 (NIV)

Holy Spirit brings Comfort. It caused me to see the importance of *every decision* must be made with the Holy Spirit. God wants to lead you and me into a deeper place of His Intimacy. He wants us to listen for His Will and His Ways. I continually asked myself am I hearing from Him. Am I *bearing fruit* for Him? (**Matthew 7:20**) Your very life will reveal your fruit. Double down on pressing in and forward with your journey. Make it the first thing you think about waking and the last thought before sleep comes. Doors of understanding began to *open*. (**Revelations 3:7**) **Stop and read this.** The Lord asks each of us to steward in purity and with clean hearts. The deeper we go, the more the Holy Spirit guides and participates, seeking us to repent. Repentance as my cleanser coupled with the Blood of the Lamb becomes my protection for me to *serve and obey* as God's Servant, God's Kitchener. God's Epistle. All with confidence to be a channel for the Kingdom coming. Be the servant example.

"I am the sprouting vine and you're my branches. As you live in union with me as your source, fruitfulness will stream from within you—but when you live separated from me you are powerless."

—John 15:5 (TPT)

TAKING ACTION TO SERVE BEARS FRUIT.
TRASH TO TREASURE

My stewardship came alive bearing fruit. I just never thought of bearing fruit before until I understood the **John 15** message. I always enjoy doing things for people. Yet, now, quiet acts of kindness to serve the Lord doubles my joy! I began to expand ways to bring happiness to my neighbors and friends. (**Galatians 6:10**) My latest idea I call Friday Roses Day when I deliver a dozen red roses to someone on Fridays! I pick up trash on the beach walks. Years ago, I picked up the trash around my neighborhood, usually Monday mornings. I recall living briefly in Boca Raton, FL, where I continued serving in this way. One day, finding a discarded rug on a busy street, I was dragging it to a nearby dumpster along with a stuffed bag of discarded items when a car full of boys drove by, throwing papers out the window, littering the street while laughing at me going by.

I think about those boys, bless them, and wonder how life for them is going today. Are they bearing fruit? I just don't understand how people don't see and realize their actions bring reactions, and repercussions Never be fooled, God, sees all. (**Hebrews 4:13**) In my small Kansas hometown, trash just didn't happen. Then another time in Chilmark, MA, where we had a home, my hubby and I picked up trash on the Crossroads and down into the Menemsha, a fishing village. Near the fish market picking up stuff one Monday in July, I found a one-hundred-dollar bill!!! I was in the local news column that week with my find! The headline read: *It Pays to Pick up Trash!* Maybe there is more prophetic meaning here!!

I remember my Trash Days in my old Ft. Lauderdale neighborhood. To this day, I have a discarded plaque I found on a Monday clean-up, now placed at the entrance of my home with (**Joshua 1:9**) *"The Lord is* *with you wherever you go."* Someone's trash became my *treasure."* After we moved and some years later, I drove through that area, seeing no debris. Wow, I thought to myself. I stopped to greet a former neighbor who told me I had started a good thing keeping the streets clean. Now, she shared with me," I carry on for you." Hearing that confirmed fruits! We become the Lord's hands and feet, manifesting His Words of encouragement for others as well as setting examples. Serving others brings joy. (**Galatians 6:2**) *Bearing fruit brings an avalanche of understanding all from one concept: Obedience.* We begin the action by developing the Fruits of *love, joy, peace, forbearance, kindness, goodness, faithfulness, gentleness, and self-control.* Love and self-control are the bookends. These are the Fruits of the Holy Spirit. Begin with these. (**John 15:5**) A good family rule: if you see you do it. The Lord asks us to become doers of the Word. Serve to bear fruit. Fruits come from giving your heart to the Lord. Fruits expand with being Born from Above, offering Eternal Life. Born into a New Everlasting Life places you immediately in the now moment. Serving others creates a *living union* with God, the Father, and a fellowship with Christ. (**1 Corinthians 15:58**) The Holy Spirit then takes over, directing you with your next steps. Give yourself to the Lord.

"But the fruit of the Spirit is love, joy, peace, forbearance, kindness, goodness faithfulness, gentleness and self-control. Against such things there is no law."

—Galatians 5:22-23 (NIV)

A living union with Christ requires receptivity. What must I learn to steward in obedience? This begins in my home with my beloved partner and family. Being receptive to my partner embraces a living union with him. My fellowship must include being responsible for myself. Obedience to Him opens the door to His Blessings over my life. My attitude towards everything manifests the way I view my life. Guard my lips in how to speak, what to say, and what to think. A living union calls me to be accountable for my emotions. My choices reveal both feelings and attitudes about what I do with my life. Seeing Christ in me becomes my goal. Let my yes be a yes. Yes, to serving God and having no guilt to say no to the world. Being grounded in the Lord means His Joy overrides and guides. (**John 15:5**) Apart from Him, I can do nothing.

Hearing the voice of God activates your soul's accountability. It is life changing. Learning to listen with obedience must follow. *Obey* with your action. A *living union* means laying on the altar of your heart what He calls you to do. As mentioned earlier, having a Spiritual Altar in your home is where you can hear from the Father. An altar allows for us to exchange with Him and receive His Power. What did Noah first do when he stepped off the Ark? Built an Altar. Invest in the Lord with your time, your resources, your talent, and treasure at your Spiritual Altar. (**Genesis 8:20**) The Father is ever watchful. When you are a new parent, your mind never leaves that child. You constantly think about that child. It is the same with Father God. He so longs for each of us to flourish in fulfilling his plans and destiny He has for us. He knit you together long before the forming of the world. (**Psalm 139:13**) He constantly leaves clues. Meet with Him in private at your altar.

My clues came in visions. It started with Holy Spirit pictures in both quiet rest and dreams of relevant objects. Recently, two white porcelain toilet bowls filled to the brim with sparkling clear water. Of course, I did what I always do, seek a dream meaning on Google. Now, Holy Spirit knows my pattern long enough to know I will do just that with whatever shows up. I loved the idea of double portion unity of greater intimacy and discernment with white for purity and clarity from the clear water. More importantly it was about getting rid of the old emotions no longer needed. How do you suppose I felt after reading this? *Powerful. Holy Spirit Power.* Another time I had a dream of the image 1496. It turned out to be a powerful Angelic Being representing a dedication for a new direction. WOW! Moving into a relationship with Yeshua revealed the supernatural Power of His Love and His Presence finally were *personal* and real. He will never forsake His Promises to me. (**Deuteronomy 31:6**)

"Be strong and courageous. Do not be afraid or terrified because of them, for the Lord you or God goes with you; he will never leave you nor forsake you."

—**Deuteronomy 31:6 (NIV)**

God is never giving up on me, nor you, my friend. God's Deep Agape Love shows up as unconditional love of a Father for His Child. So deep is this love there is never a moment you are not on His Mind. If I am rushed or even a little anxious driving somewhere I repeat my favorite mantra: *God is taking care of me.* He wants you to know Him. (**Matthew 28:20**) The more time spent in understanding the spiritual giftings devotes your heart to know Him more deeply. The more time spent to know the Father, the more you will trust the Father. Every time you study scripture, you will know Him more deeply. Devote yourself to unfolding the Fruits of the Spirit to develop the Gifts of the Spirit. When you become a *living union*, you will walk in His Peace. (**Ephesians 4:3**) Peace gives you a renewal of your spirit. Holy Spirit longs for a deeply personal relationship with us.

"But the fruit of the Spirit is love, joy, peace, forbearance, kindness, goodness faithfulness, gentleness and self-control. Against such things there is no law."

—**Galatians 5:22-23** (NIV)

"If the Spirit is the source of our life, we much also allow the Spirit to direct every aspect of our lives."

—Galatians 5:25 (TPT)

Holy Spirit helped me to know the Lord God loves my beloved more than I do. He knows him and knows what he needs. He is a child of God as well. He knows his heart and how to soften it. Finally, I was able to see I am not to judge anything. Only the Lord offers the final judgment on all things. I soon began to understand the enemy on many occasions causing the difficulties, not my partner. The thief comes to destroy the one I love because he does not want me to grow spiritually. **(John 10:10)** From this perspective, I began to have greater obedience in my walk with the Lord and a greater understanding and compassion for the behavior I was seeing. I discovered I could stop judging and cease any unkind responses to smooth the atmosphere with forbearance. Just being with my beloved with no plan was suddenly important, more than ever before. Holy Spirit led me stop judging and start loving.

STOP JUDGING, KEEP LOVING, STAY SILENT

From this perspective, the closer my walk with the Holy Spirit, the greater my compassion releases my judgments. Remember, an unbeliever does not understand the trustworthiness of the Lord. Every morning He offers fresh mercies for a new day and a clean slate. A believer understands that only the Father and Creator of the heavens and the earth acts as the Righteous Judge. **(1 Corinthians 4:5)** This passage tells us to judge nothing before the appointed time; wait until the Lord comes when he brings to light the hidden things of darkness. We must be careful not to judge lest we be judged accordingly. With this understanding, silence became my friend. It is hard to stop the carnal mind from criticizing. Stop thinking and start investing in your partner with your time and acts of kindness (**Titus 3:4-5**) The greater the investment results in a beautiful blessing. I bless my partner and our marriage with these insight as I turn to prayer.

"Finally, all of you be like-minded be sympathetic, love one another, be compassionate and humble. Do not repay evil with evil or insult with insult. On the contrary, repay evil with blessing, because to this you were called so that you may inherit a blessing."

—1 Peter 3:8-9 (NIV)

SCRIPTURE AND INTERCESSION PRAYER WITH HOT COALS

Despite knowing my partner did not want to discuss the Lord, I followed my heart in understanding his behavior from a higher perspective. Suddenly I was so grateful for my prayer groups. It is good to seek out followers of Christ to stand in agreement in prayer. Daily study of the scriptures leads us to open the door to faith and trust in the Lord's Promises. Reading the Word gives us clarity to cleanse away unbelief and mistrust. Prayer increases the holiness in life. Join others in devotion to serving the Kingdom through interceding for others. A commitment to intercessory prayer must be deep and very personally aligned with the Lord. (**1 Timothy 2:1**) Ask the Holy Spirit to send you thoughts of who is needing pray. You must obey. More prayer brings more incredible Holy Spirit Power to your prayers. Prepare to grow in the Body of Christ through worship and intercession. With prayer partners, what you bind on earth will be bound in Heaven. What you loose on the earth is loosed in Heaven. Become a Hot Coal for Jesus!

"Truly I tell you, whatever you bind on earth will be bound in heaven, and whatever you loose on earth will be loosed in heaven. Again, truly I tell you if two of you on earth agree about anything they ask for, it will be done for them by my Father in Heaven. For where two or more gather in my name, there am I with them."

—Matthew 18:18-20 (NIV)

God has blessed me with prayer partners. Meeting to pray together every week assures and inspires my prayer with more incredible passion. (**James 5:13-15**) Prayers of Faith brings unity to Hot Coals for the Lord! The Faithful Four meet weekly by phone for intercessory prayer and calls as needed. They are a part of my trusted prophetic circle. Another is a Cypress-based Middle Eastern intercessory prayer partners to assist with the Rapid Church Planting of Apostle Guenther Hess in Europe, Africa, Asia, and the Middle East. Fridays, the prayer group meets for Israel. The *Give Him 15* daily word of Dutch Sheets calls us to pray with his intercessor team for America. Clay Nash has weekly and daily calls with intercessors all over the country. Intercessors for America send daily emails for prayer needs. Hot Coals. Seek the Holy Spirit to find your prayer calling. It will strengthen your resolve to serve the Lord. Create time to hear the Word for global needs and time to hear personally from the Lord. Quiet time will bring you peace to deepen your Inner Spirit.

Step by step my Inner Spirit shifted. After I was baptized from above by the Holy Spirit, I embraced water baptism on several occasions to release and die to myself for birth new into the Life of Christ. I no longer live, but Christ lives in me. (**Galatians 2:20**) I remember thinking about receiving the Holy Spirit Language and how that would happen. Speaking with a trusted spiritual mentor about this, I released any concern and trusted one day it would come. I am a believer in short naps to restore my soul. My eyes let me know when a nap is needed. So, this specific day I headed off for a nap. Such a welcome feeling came over me as I drifted off. Sure enough, when I least expected it, I awoke speaking in tongues. (**1 Corinthians 14:1**) Over time this has changed. One day at my woman's club meeting I was having difficulty with my computer and automatically went into tongues without being aware of it. One of the gals nearby heard me. She thought it sounded Korean! Wow! I asked her if she knew that language. No, it just sounds like it. Slipping into tongues solved a problem only Holy Spirit would know how to fix. Isn't it true that the Lord wants us to *Auto Respond* to him? Those present would not understand the words of our prayers, for we would be praying in our spirit language. Imagine the Father's ability to hear from millions of souls at the same time. He knows and listens. I embrace these prayers in my *Spirit Language to produce much fruit.* Blessings in the Spirit are especially for when we don't know how to pray from something. We are the remnant, the chosen ones. Tongues restore us. Napping in the Spirit awakens us to the mind of Christ. The more we speak in tongues, the more we allow the Holy Spirit to speak life and faith into us taking our prayers to the Father. Speaking in tongues edifies you. (**1 Corinthians 14:2**) Not only this, speaking in tongues offers worship to the Father, guidance from the Holy Spirit, and can become a weapon when dealing with the enemy. (**Acts 10:46**) Prayers in tongues magnifies God through the Holy Spirit Power.

"But you will receive power when the Holy Spirit comes on you and you will be my witnesses in Jerusalem and in all Judea and Samaria and to the ends of the earth."

—Acts 1:8 (NIV)

"The person without the Spirit does not accept the things that come from the Spirit of God but consider them foolishness, and cannot understand them because they are discerned only through the Spirit."

—1 Corinthians 2:14 (NIV)

The Living Bible (TLB) puts it like this:

"But the man who isn't a Christian cannot understand and can't accept these thoughts from God, which the Holy Spirit teaches us. They sound foolish to him, because only those who have the Holy Spirit within them can understand what the Holy Spirit means."

"Follow the way of love and eagerly desire gifts of the Spirit, especially prophecy. For anyone who speaks in a tongue does not speak to people but to God. Indeed, no one understands them; they utter mysteries by the Spirit."

—1 Corinthians 14:1-3 (NIV)

PRAYING IN THE SPIRIT

Praying in tongues will add to the power to your spiritual life. A Holy Spirit baptism will bring the gift of a heavenly language. I enjoyed the Empower 2000 Series with Apostle Donald Lee entitled "Warfare that Works." He spoke about his recent best-selling book *Tongues Power & Blessings*. His motto is: "Much prayer, much power. Some prayer, some violence, Little prayer, little power. No prayer, no power." Praying in the Spirit will enhance not only your Holy Spirit-led wisdom, will bring new and fresh revelation to grow. Tongues will help you know the hope of your calling. There is an *incomparable power* given to the believer who regularly speaks in tongues. I promise you tongues, the language of the Spirit, opens doors to enhance your life and your ability to serve Christ wherever you go. It enlarges your faith to new levels! It allows for protection as well as transforming our weaknesses into strengths. It enhances your personality. The Fire of the Holy Spirit can purify us of our faults with His consuming fire. As we pray fervently in tongues, the Holy Spirit brings us transformational gifts of joy! More prayers, more joy!!!

"Suddenly a sound like the blowing of a violent wind came from heaven and filled the whole house where they were sitting. They saw what seemed to be tongues of fire that separated and came to rest on each of them. All of them were filled the Holy Spirit and began to speak in other tongues as the Spirit enabled them."

—Acts 2:2-4 (NIV)

"I keep asking that the God of our Lord Jesus Christ the glorious Father, may give you the Spirit of wisdom and revelation, so that you may know him better. I pray that the eyes of your heart may be enlightened in order that you may now the hope to which has called you, the riches of his glorious inheritance in his holy people, and his incomparably great power for us who believe."

—Ephesians 1:17-19 (NIV)

"...because God hath from the beginning chose you as first fruits to be saved through sanctification of the Spirit and belief of the truth."

—2 Thessalonians 2:13 (NIV)

"I pray that out of his glorious riches he may strengthen you with power through the Spirit in your inner being so that Christ may dwell in your hearts through faith."

—Ephesians 3:16-17 (NIV)

Add grace to your obedience and prayers with fasting. Fasting will increase your receptivity to the Lord's voice and His Word. Fasting will invite the Holy Spirit to do more intense work in you. The Jewish people fast from Sundown to the next Sundown. A 24-hour fast is a good place to start. Eat Breakfast, then no more food until the next morning's Breakfast. There are many examples of fasts in the bible, such as the Esther 3 Day Fast. There is water only fasts as well. Those who need to be cautious might drop something from their daily intake to signify their intention. Fasting can break off oppression. (**Isaiah 58:6**) The goal of fasting is to deepen spiritual awareness with hunger pangs as of a reminder to pray. Fasting will lift your burdens and put your heart into a new place. (**Ezra 8:23**) Fasting will strengthen your joy to make it astonishing. Do not make your fasting obvious with others. It is for the Father to see your *obedience and devotion*. It is for you to serve the Father. Become His Steward.

"When you fast, don't let it be obvious, but instead, wash your face and groom yourself and realize that your Father in the secret is the one who is watching all that you do in secret and will continue to reward you."

—Matthew 6:17-18 (TPT)

STEWARDSHIP ANOINTS ACTION

Obedience creates Absolute Surrender. Stewardship takes the Holy Spirit anointing into action. Just look at Abraham and his son Isaac. The Lord put his servant's faith, and loyalty to the supreme test with the *"Ram is in the Bush."* The saving of Isaac was the ultimate demonstration of the kind of obedience God requires. (**Genesis 22: 1-14**) He and Sarah left their home without knowing their destination. Utter and Absolute surrender into the hands of God's Infinite Love deepens complete trust in God's Unfailing Power. He believed the promises of generations to follow would be more than all the stars and all the sand by the sea. I look at my life's tests. Sometimes I tell myself: *The Ram is in the Bush.* Just imagine how Abraham must have felt. Abraham rested in faith and belief of God's Words in his Covenant Promise. (**Romans 4:13**) Through righteousness that comes by faith, Abraham became the Father of the Nations because he obeyed. Even though Abraham made errors in judgement, his Covenant Promise was held through his faith. Therefore, the promise comes by faith to us as well so that it may be by grace guaranteed to multiply. Yes, the Ram is in the Bush. His faith and trust gave him the needed rest. Abraham knew God. He feared God. Abraham believed in God's Word, and he obeyed without argument. Finally, he surrendered his will to God. God had tested Abraham for desiring to be a father. Finally, after 100 years of waiting for a child and Sarah at age 95, a son Isaac was given. Imagine it. Let each of us grow to soar in discerning what we need to do in our personal surrender to the Father.

Surrender to the Father to change the atmosphere. To flourish in our lives, we must come to an understanding *we can do nothing ourselves.* Yet, we can do it all with the Lord God. Let us make our surrender and obedience like a perfume we spoke of earlier to change the atmosphere wherever we go! Let us decree daily we receive a miracle as well as become a miracle to someone! Wherever you go, remember you are changing the atmosphere! The bible is full of testimonies where instantly God's Hand was moving over a situation like young David and the Huge Philistine Goliath yelling down at him. David threw the stone for *God to hit the mark!* Just for fun, google a map of Israel around 700-900 BC and just see where Israel, Judah, and the Philistines were located. Close your eyes and march out on the field with David. He had long been prepared to kill bears and lions to protect His Sheep. He knew the Hand of the Lord instructed every move to make rescuing his sheep. (**1 Samuel 17:45**) That is the stuff of testimonies! *You have the same stuff* creating a legacy testimony with your newly acquired Holy Spirit. Goliath must have been enraged over David's handsome beauty!

Let's all decide to reveal how we *love God* through our obedience! You are so very powerful when you choose to own your *irrevocable gifts.* (**Romans 11:29**) There has never been another *you.* There will never be another *now.* This is not to become famous; instead, to realize the power and beauty you carry. Pray. Declare. Prepare. Shift. Practice this daily, even at the grocery store and the gas station! Before you shop, stop, and pray. Declare and expect discernment to shift with calling forth God's Favor in all things and with all people. (**Psalm 5:12**) Show the Holy Spirit through your actions and word you desire to make a shift. Seek to be with others already shifting!!! When you see how the Power of the Holy Spirit can work with you, a *power surge* takes hold of you. This is what happens when you answer the call to reach out in fellowship. Reach out to your partner in a fresh way.

"I have been crucified with Christ and I no longer live, but Christ lives in me. The life I now live in the body, I live by faith in the Son of God, who loved me and gave himself for me."

—Galatians 2:20 (NIV)

"I find that the strength of Christ's explosive power infuses me to conquer every difficulty. For I can do everything through Christ, who gives me strength."

—Philippians 4:13 (TPT)

"But seek first His Kingdom and His Righteousness and all these things will be given to you as well."

—Matthew 6:33 (NIV)

A church is not a place; it is a body with blood ties to Jesus Christ. God calls us to be the Ecclesia which is His Governing Body for His Kingdom Glory. We are called to do what Jesus came to do, bring the Good News to those around us. He came to restore His Father's Kingdom. Dr. Francis Myles in his book, *The Order of Melchizedek*, reminds us Jesus didn't go to the cross to birth a religion. Christ died for our sins becoming our sins and more importantly to bring to the Eternal Spiritual Order of Kingly Priests through the Order of Melchizedek, the Royal Priesthood of Jesus Christ. Christ brings to us a great transition from religious christianity to the Kingdom Principles. This is a life-changing concept. Where we gather becomes a Kingdom House of God. A living house where His Chosen People gather. **(Romans 12:15-16)** Consider a Home Church with like-minded believers where you can participate in the Kingdom's Body of Christ with your gifts. (**1 Corinthians 12:13**) The Kingdom Teachings of the Order of Melchizedek are spreading rapidly throughout the world. It was in the Valley of the Kings, the trading floor for Kingdom business that Melchizedek met with Abraham to bless him with the first communion. (**Genesis 14:18**) Jesus is the High Priest of the Order of Melchizedek. Jesus carries the Glory of the Father. (**Read Hebrews 7**)

Apostle Guenther Hess of the RCP, standing for Rapid Church Planting, follows Christ Great Commission to create disciples worldwide. His Home Church training currently embraces equipping and transforming Africa. The Lord called Him to bring revival to Africa. He did not go the route of staying in larger cities with comfort. No, he went to the small villages beginning with Rwanda, Uganda, then Tanzania, then Kenya where conditions were extreme. No official roads. Yet, he persisted in attracting to him others wanting to serve the Kingdom. Now, his online Timothy Bible Schools are bringing in the harvest, with hundreds being saved daily. This is where the Heart of the Father gives multiplication to His servants. He gives him Favor because Guenther has put aside himself to answer only to the Lord with radical obedience. Miracles are underway in Europe and Africa. Apostle Hess has been to over 65 nations with his Home Church Planting. There is an explosion of God's Consuming Fire in these nations! Praise God!

Put on Christ with praise and prayer. Experience Jesus through fellowship in prayer. As believers we are called to pray. (**Romans 8:28**) Fellowship with the Lord multiplies and expands us. We all need guidance to know what to release and what to claim and embrace. What matters is the *Holy Spirit Presence* offering discernment as an answer. For me, prayer is the answer. (**1Thessalonians 5:16-18**) Pray continuously over all circumstances! His Living Word is the Answer that reveals His Will for you. *Prayer partners are the answer.* How else could I anticipate the Kingdom coming except to know I am the Kingdom and part of the Body of Christ. I do this for my family. I take a stand now over what I will say and do. I pray for larger issues and the smallest of things. I put on Christ wearing a cross daily.

This cross is a part of my fabric as it was a gift from my husband for our 25th Wedding Anniversary, a lovely memory.

When I was a young girl, my mother made me a Dress Up Box with her dresses, high heels, hats, purses, gloves, and pearls. Oh, I loved to dress up and still do. Between my playhouse and playing dress up I could spend hours alone. Now I look back to see I covered myself to feel special. That is what prayer does. It covers yourself to feel the Presence of the Lord. Clothe yourself in prayer. I say no without guilt to the world and yes to embrace my Lord with prayer. I keep my eyes fixed on the Lord, who is returning very soon. It is time to prepare your life. My prayer life is my godly life that develops my Holy Character intimacy with Christ. Daily, decree blessings over your partner, your family, and your life. Ask for the Favor of God over your relationships to multiply and grow. **Psalm 91 Prayers** for my marriage became God's Umbrella for the storms. It gives me comfort, and it will work for you as well. Through each of us God's Kingdom is coming to earth as it is in Heaven. May you find joy to seek the Lord in obedience.

"Whoever dwells in the shelter of the Most High will rest in the shadow of the Almighty." I will say of the Lord, "He is my refuge and my fortress, my God in whom I trust."

—Psalm 91:1-2 (NIV)

TIME TO SIT WITH THE LORD TO JOURNAL AND REFLECT.

Be so serious about asking God for ideas for your life. Begin with praise to the Lord.

- Why is it important to be with others who are on fire for the Lord? Is there someone (friend) who encourages you spiritually?

- Does your spouse attend a place of worship with you? Is your spouse jealous of the time with the Lord?

- Do you participate in a prayer group? Are you actively in prayer with the Lord?

- Ask the Lord to show you where to find fellowship with like-minded people.

- Take time daily to write down and read aloud your gratitude, thanksgiving, and Joy! Thank Him for your spiritual growth to deepen your obedience.

- Do you rejoice? *Rejoice Always!* Are you praying over everything?

DECLARATION: I place my trust in you, Jesus, to reveal my next step with my partner. I will seek opportunities to grow in the gifts of the spirit

REFLECT ON THE FOLLOWING AND WRITE YOUR THOUGHTS IN YOUR PRAYER JOURNAL:

- YOUR THOUGHTS TO JESUS

- IDEAS AND WORDS FROM JESUS

PRAYER: *Precious Lord Jesus, I come to you today to greet you with the Joy that you have given me. I welcome the day with the expectation of a miracle in my marriage. Lord, I thank you for my prayer partners and the encouragement I receive there. I move forward to deepen my spiritual maturity with prayers for others. I seek to be your steward, Lord, to encourage my partner and my family with their heart's desire because I know Lord you are placing in them your call for their purpose. Lord God, I choose to praise you in the face of adversity, knowing your power has an anointing over my life and my family. Thank you, Jesus, for blessing me with the Obedience to find your peace and fresh mercy every day. In Jesus Precious Name, Amen.*

Chapter 3
PURITY

Thy Will be Done on Earth as it is in Heaven.

SIFT AND SHIFT YOUR UNION WITH HUMILITY

CHEF NOTE: One of the secrets to cooking I discovered was the importance of the purity of the ingredients. Freshness. I guess eggs come to mind first. Farm Eggs scream freshness so vastly different than those sitting in the grocery for who knows how long. Growing up in a small Kansas community, we had our own chickens and thus, fresh eggs on demand! Just ask my mother, who was the Queen of Angel Food Cakes! What's not to love; cakes from the angels! In fact, she baked these cakes for all sorts of occasions. In my small Kansas hometown, being neighborly and kind meant taking food for a death in the family, as well as a celebration. So, okay…the eggs. Well, mom used eggs from our own chickens! She always used 12 eggs. So, when she baked one of her cakes, the rule was *"Don't slam the door"* causing it to fall. WOW, fresh eggs make such a difference. Mom's angel food cakes came from heaven. In searching for her recipes, which are my treasure, I found this basic recipe. Honestly, I think she just did it from memory. My husband called my first angel food cake attempt "Fallen Angel Food Cake!" I will continue testing recipes, commit them to memory and share just like Mom. It is rather humbling to create a *fallen cake!* Forgive me, Mother if I use a box cake mix! It will still be to honor your beautiful intentions.

Thus, humility becomes the ingredient of purity. God searches worldwide, looking for those who steward others with clean hands and pure, humble hearts. He seeks those whose members with eyes, ears, mouths, hands, and feet consciously dedicate themselves to righteous living. Purity of mind. Let's look at how humility can be crucial to purity in our cake and in our lives.

CO-CREATE WITH HOLY SPIRIT—LISTENING AND DOING

My first recollection of listening was with my friend Nancy. Two great memories of Nancy are she had a cat clock in her bedroom with a tail that ticked the minutes and eyes that went back and forth, and her aunt was the local telephone operator for Holyrood, my hometown. Her Aunt Vera's tiny office was above the Holyrood Gazette, who published weekly the hometown news! Up the stairs, we would go. Now, in Holyrood, you could have a private line or be on a party line. The telephones were wall units with a crank. To reach anyone, you had to go through Aunt Vera. Wow, this so dates me! We would go visit her aunt and listen. Just loved listening to the party line especially. Well, it is that way with the Holy Spirit. We need to listen only to the Holy Spirit for what to do next. Instruction. We need discernment to tune out other voices to become awakened. Remember, you have a *private line* with Holy Spirit!

"My dear brothers and sisters, take note of this: Everyone should be quick to listen, slow to speak and slow to become angry because human anger does not produce the righteousness that God desires."

—James 1:19-20 (NIV)

Holy Spirit awakened me to my need for humility, conviction, and correction to have purity of heart. It meant I needed to clean the soil of my heart to see with the eyes of my heart. It is cleaning your lenses to see clearly how the Lord uses you for His Purposes. It means becoming enlightened to know He has plans for you. (**Jeremiah 29:11**) How can you become aware of the Lord's Plans? We wait on God to reveal His Will through His Holy Spirit. Through our waiting and with day-by-day reflection, Holy Spirit will bring us ideas and thoughts. (**Revelation 3:22**) It caused me to honestly look at everything about myself, including my flaws and, most notably, my attitude about my partner.

I asked the Lord to show me the flawed personality traits that needed shifting for my walk with Him. God uses our flaws to equip us for His Calling on our lives. Only through the flaws of brokenness can God begin to help us understand *humility*. Asher Intrater in his book *Authority* tells us it begins with being broken; broken of every thought that we can accomplish something with our own ability. We must come to a place of knowing we ourselves can do nothing without the Father's Son. This draws to us the need for humility, to remain low, to be a servant to the Father in all things. Daily, I pray for my self-absorption to be removed and my pride to be revealed. Show me, Holy Spirit, any self-centeredness to be removed from me. This is the pruning process which can be so difficult. Every single soul has a calling on their life. Jesus waits patiently for the awakening to begin the equipping for a greater spiritual understanding even with simple common-sense things.

"...to equip his people for works of service, so that the body of Christ may be built up until we reach unity in the faith and in the knowledge of the Son of God and become mature, attaining to the whole measure of the fullness of Christ."

—Ephesians 4:12 (NIV)

Holy Spirit offers comfort. Being tall (did I mention this?) complicates things. I learned quickly not to tower over people in conversations making them uncomfortable. Seated ones were far more fruitful. He shows us how to best align with the Lord in mind. I recall a time when my daughter was very young. She loved sitting in the cart moving all around the grocery store! My best helper! Nearby, I heard a young boy yell to his mother, *"Mama, look at the giant lady."* I looked around to see the giant lady and discovered it was me. Sometimes, I forget who I am. Being made tall was surely part of the Lord's Plan for me. The Lord will show each of us how best to use our gifts. All our attributes become part of our identity in Him. Because we were both tall, God made it possible to meet my Beloved Husband, my partner.

Holy Spirit reminds us, who we are and how to carry ourselves. Interchanges become God opportunities! I thank the Holy Spirit conviction helping to recall the many times I stepped off the path, Holy Spirit will show me these areas when I intentionally seek to know them. For example, not listening and even interrupting people seemed to plague me. Talking over people reflects self-importance. Oh pride, let you be released now. (**Proverbs 16:18**) The correction was painful. These corrections would not be audible, rather, a still small voice within. The Holy Spirit's conviction can feel so heavy, yet so necessary for us to see when we step into the identity of being in Christ and away from identifying with the flesh. (**John 13:33**) Holy Spirit calls to remind us to step into showing the love of the Father.

My Inner Spirit awakened quickly to sense the need for repentance. (**Acts 3:19-20**) Especially words were spoken in anger which cannot be retrieved. Those hurtful words are like a stone thrown in the lake; you don't see how deep down it goes to wound. It calls for us to listen for these corrections from Holy Spirit and, likewise, become the listener for the Lord. Becoming a listener fosters our need to surrender ourselves completely to hear from Him. (**James 4:7**) A quiet strength of the Lord began to take over my being. Make sure you allow this listening skill to grow with your partner. Make sure he feels you are hearing him, listening with you heart to hear his.

Listening reveals the greatest gift of humility you can give to others. I needed to learn to allow the silence that comes sometimes and resist trying to fill it with my thoughts. Be quick to listen and slow to speak. (**James 1:19**). A person of humility listens to *honor the Christ in another.* Jesus listened to others. Jesus mastered the art of listening with uninterrupted attention. I am reminded of Dr. Joseph Peck who listens with Holy Spirit ears to what you have to say always giving a pause before speaking. Jesus also took the time necessary to listen to others. He was *never in a hurry.* Listen with Holy Spirit Ears. This correction opens the doors to serving the Lord. I am so grateful to receive a penalty from my loving Father. Until recent years, I didn't even *know* the word repentance. Repentance brings forth the fruit of righteousness. Daily in communion, I repent for yesterday's action I might have missed. *I am so thankful the Lord loves me enough to correct me* and forgives me with shed blood which also cleanses. Repentance is the beginning of moving into humility. The Holy Spirit will let you know, believe me, and it can be humbling.

"Listen, my son, accept what I say, and the years of your life will be many. I instruct you in the way of wisdom and lead you along straight paths."

—Proverbs 10-11 (NIV)

"My dearest brothers and sisters take this to heart. Be quick to listen but slow to speak. And be slow to become angry, for human anger is never a legitimate tool to promote God's righteous purpose."

—James 1:19-20 (TPT)

MAKE HUMILITY YOUR TEACHING TOOL

Humility is the secret to making your Heart Sing. Walking in humility causes your family and those around you to become aware of something shifting. You shift in your actions, responses, kindness (sincere), and willingness to serve, which quietly alerts them! Maybe you even learn to slow down with them to stop rushing without hearing or seeing their needs. They sense something about you without knowing what has changed and probably with a bit of suspect. (**1 James 5:6-7**) Andrew Murray, in his book, *Humility & Absolute Surrender,* tells us, "We shall find that the deepest humility is the secret of the truest happiness, of a joy that nothing can destroy." Jesus in whom we trust can make us humble. Let us accept all that humbles us as Christ comes to us in our weakness. Your humility becomes a reflective mirror for your partner. *Your humility will unlock the enemy's hold on a person's heart.* You might even begin to see sincere appreciation coming from the formerly locked lips of your beloved. It will unlock your heart to sing as well! Sing to yourself in a private moment with the Lord. Being married to an unbeliever creates the perfect opportunity for humility to be a weapon of change! Give praise often!

MAKE PRAISE YOUR NEW WEAPON

Praise becomes a glorious blessing. *Take your position to use the weapon of Praise to the Lord!* (**Exodus 15:2**) *When you praise your partner, you are literally praising the Lord within him!* Humility will help you steward your marriage in a new direction. Humility can be a turning of the tide in a relationship. My partner feels the Presence of the Lord by the acts of kindness I sincerely offer. Taking time with those you love gifts them in a way no other can. Giving your time to those you love, making their agenda first, will make your heart sing. It shows you are all in for God. Yeshua desires you to share His heart for every single person you meet. It makes His Heart sing! *This is the secret* of making *your* heart sing as well. God has given us different kinds of spiritual weapons to use. *The Word is a double-edged sword!* (**Hebrews 4:12**) His Living Word can be a blessing and a weapon against the enemy. They are more powerful than any physical weapon of this world with which we might do battle. (**2 Corinthians 10:4**) Your prayers, with His Word rise to the Bowls in Heaven to be tipped out upon the situation! Heavenly sent answers will cause you to praise the Lord! Praise as a weapon might seem unnatural, but it is *supernatural*. Your Praise becomes the Lord's blessing. Soak in His Presence with your Praise to receive His Fountain of Living Waters. He will rejoice over your fellowship and dependence on Him.

"I have always trusted in your kindness, so answer me. I will spin a circle of joy when you or salvation lifts me up."

—Psalm 13:5 (TPT)

"It s is good to praise the Lord and make music to your name; oh most High; proclaiming your love in the morning and your faithfulness at night."

—Psalm 92:1-2 (NIV)

God requires complete dependence on Him. Humility causes us to look to the Lord for His Hand to be over our concerns. It is utter and absolute dependence upon God. It is impossible to walk the way of humility (**Micah 6:8**) without looking entirely to God to show us what to do in each circumstance. We seek His Heart to lead our heart. The more you do this, the greater it becomes, the more Holy Spirit will guide us! Through the Holy Spirit Comforter, we are led to the Lord Jesus's heart. When you are walking in the Presence of the Lord, plans can suddenly change, causing confusion. Yet, with obedience, you will find the change to be remarkable. Look less with frustration on sudden changes and more with praise and thanksgiving. It is paying attention to that still small voice that awakens you to reorder your steps.

Thank goodness for the still small voice of the Holy Spirit! I had plans to leave one morning to go to the laundromat to wash an oversize bedspread which would take time. That small still voice said tomorrow. I switched my plans to stay home, thank goodness I did. I had forgotten that day was the final walk-through of the property we were leaving. Thinking it was the next day, I saved myself a disaster. Holy Spirit knows your calendar better than you do! Depend on Him to help you find freedom. (**2 Corinthians 3:17**) When you walk daily with the Holy Spirit, He begins to understand and recognize your weakness. That keeps you looking to the Lord for your Strength. (**Isaiah 12:2**) Abundant life is trusting in Him without fear. It is living in continual dependence on Him. (**2 Corinthians 9:8**) Looking back, you will see it always gets done more quickly in the way of the Lord. Humility is saying yes, Lord, have it your way. Father knows best by setting you free to enjoy Him and His Plans for you.

"He has shown you, a mortal, what is good. And what does the Lord require of you? To act justly to love mercy and to walk humbly with your God."

—Micah 6:8 (NIV)

"With tender humility and quiet patience always demonstrate gentleness and generous love toward on another especially toward those who may try your patience."

—Ephesians 4:2 (TPT)

"Within your heart you can make plans for your future, but the Lord chooses the steps you take to get there."

—Proverbs 16:9 (TPT)

Humility helps you stay in your lane. Lord, discipline me to try and try again to remember and know my identity in you. Help me to stay in my lane with discernment for what to do and not to do. Avoid judging others, my friend, to stay in your lane. (**Matthew 7:12**) False humility comes from that place where you act from your self-importance. You know a better kind of thing. Time and time again, I catch myself in the judgment of my partner over something. Thank you, Jesus, for the Holy Spirit's conviction. This calls me to grow spiritually and awaken to my role. Being perfectly loved is the very best understanding to embrace. Jesus loves my partner more than I do. He reminds me to continue my loving while he continues His Healing, His Deliverance. Being faithful to Jesus with humility and praise will literally alter the atmosphere wherever you go, and with whomever you share. Stay in your lane. A lane of humility becomes the way God will move over your marriage. It will accomplish what confrontation cannot do. Show the Father's Love. Yes, humility teaches like no other.

"God has transmitted his very Substance into every Scripture, for it is God-breathed. It will empower you by its instruction and correction, giving you the strength to take the right direction and lead you deeper into the path of godliness. Then you will be God's servant, fully mature and perfectly prepared to fulfill any assignment God gives you."

—2 Timothy 3:15-17 (TPT)

"Be willing to be made low before the Lord and he will exalt you!"

—James 4:10 (TPT)

Think about purity of the heart. Purity means being pure. Pure can mean being free from impurities, full-strength or even containing nothing inappropriate like pure chocolate! We can all relate to chocolate. The higher the purity the greater the taste. In the same way the Lord Loves purity of your heart (**Proverbs 22:11**) The greater we move away from stepping off the path the more our lives will be blessed making our hearts sing with joy! *You can move from brokenness to wholeness in your heart with Jesus.* He gives us strength in our weakness to release iniquities of wrong thinking and doing. God loves us so much; he removes those things that hinder our walk with him. Discipline shows the way to making a shift in the purity of our humility. God is calling us to serve our partners, our families and those on our path. Humility offers a way for us to be the Good Samaritan in our own home. (**Luke 10: 25-37**) I was so very touched by my Beloved Mother's care of others. After my father passed away it was too difficult, especially in the winters for mother to live alone. My brother and I were so grateful for the beautiful neighbors who helped her. The day came for us to sell our childhood home. The auction was set up right in our yard with trailers of tools, kitchen things and personal things too. Mom went that night to the Ellsworth Nursing Home. It was crushing to do this, yet best. On a return visit just a month later, there was mother helping a lady in her wheelchair. This was so like my mother. It causes me to cry just thinking about the humility and lovely nature of her heart. She answered a call. It is a call to stop what we are doing to see what is needed, then give what you can at that moment. Give your time. Serving others becomes the Lord's Hands and Feet on the ground. Holy Spirit Conviction reminds us to ruthlessly eliminate hurry to avoid missing an opportunity to serve. Purity of your intention reveals the humility of your heart. (**Psalm 51:10**) May it be directed away from yourself to someone needing attention. Courageous humility allows God to discipline giving us a greater sensitivity to His Presence. This helps us to daily walk in His purity. He wants us to remember the impurity of pride is a loss of humility.

"Our parents corrected us for the short time of our childhood as it seemed good to them. But God corrects us throughout our lives for our own good, giving us an invitation to share his holiness. Now all discipline seems to be painful at the time, yet later it will produce a transformation of character, bringing a harvest of righteousness and peace to those who yield to it."

—Hebrews 12:10-11 (TPT)

"You are to lead by a different model if you want to be the greatest then live as one called to serve others. The path to promotion comes by having the heart of a bond-slave who serves everyone."

—Mark 10:43-44 (TPT)

"This is the one who gives his strength and might to his people. This is the Lord giving us his kiss of peace."

—Psalm 29:11 (TPT)

"Remember this if you have a lofty opinion of yourself and seek to be honored, you will be humbled. But if you have a modest opinion of yourself and choose to humble yourself you will be honored."

—Matthew 23:11-12 (TPT)

DIE TO MYSELF—SAY GOODBYE TO PRIDE

Perfect humility says goodbye to the need for perfection, another big issue. Pride foolishly gets in my way. A crushing moment came one day years ago that has never left me. I was volunteering with another gal at an organization. We were awaiting our next clients to help. I was standing at a table looking over some material and she said to me, "you must not have many friends." I turned in astonishment to ask why she would say this. "You always look so perfect." This is being brought low. Yet, the Lord was showing me something I needed to fully understand. Pride in self. Brought low to lean not on my own understanding. (**Proverbs 3:5-6**) From this I learned my own *inner pride self* creates the greatest obstacle to my spiritual maturity and maybe, for you too. I had to look at what in my partnership suffered from my being prideful. What is it about pride anyway?

Pride becomes the loss of humility which has us believe we can lean on our own understanding. Jesus came to bring humility back to earth to make us partaker of it and by it to save us. He led a life of perfect humility. His humility became our salvation. His salvation leads us to our humility.

We are heavenly beings walking an earthly life. No one is walking in perfection. No one. Only Jesus walked a blameless life. He came down from the throne room of heaven to walk a blameless life so that he would become the perfect Lamb with no imperfections to shed His Blood for our sin (**1 Thessalonians 5:23**) Only through the shed Blood of Jesus are we able to walk blameless as he took away our sin. It had to be a perfect and blameless person who died; a flawless lamb, Jesus came to bring us a New Covenant of Eternal Life. Nothing can take us from the Father. In the Mosaic Covenant days of Moses, the blood of a perfect little lamb was shed. Shed over and over because it never could take away the sin. God gave us His Perfect Son to be the one whose pure blood of the Father could save us. No more yearly sacrifices are needed only daily repentance and confession. Please the Lord with all things done in humility and to His glory to help you die daily as He cleanses you with His Shed Blood. Rejoice in the many ways He has blessed you. Just imagine God sent His Beloved Son, Jesus Christ to die for you with his shed His Blood taking on the curse of sin and darkness. It is humbling to grasp this gift of serving others. Jesus became our sin.

Humility means to serve from the lower place. It means being willing to not be recognized, to do what you see needs to be done without praise. Simply put it calls for surrender and willingness to be unnoticed, unrecognized, and not acknowledged in you work with the Lord. Give Him all Glory. It means giving the Lord your vessel and let the Potter have His Way. (**Isaiah 64:8**) It means seeking His Will, His Covenant and His Purpose for you. I do everything for His glory, not mine. Put God's glory above all else and you will be covered by it. T.H.G.A.T.G. To Him Give All the Glory.

Let's go back to the Hallandale Symphonic Orchestra. By all standards I should not have been playing in it at all with the little training I had. You can sort of hide in an orchestra. Yet, the Lord had me there, so I constantly gave Him all the glory to get me through every concert. One time during summer on Martha's Vineyard, I belonged to a small 6-7 people) sinfonietta. Again, I played second violin. We performed a concert in a church with my husband and daughter seated in the upper balcony. It all sort of fell apart and the conductor had to stop and start us again. Horrified, I feared it my fault yet, bravely, I did my best. Later my family told me we sounded like the Walter Matthau Band. Well, I did have to laugh because it was true!! I can laugh at myself and at the same time be determined to do better. Another time I played in the Chilmark Church with several other string players. Awful would best describe me. I was made low; yet, I rejoiced and gave God the Glory.

"If my people, who are called by my name, will humble themselves and pray and seek my face and turn from their wicked ways, then I will hear from heaven, and I will forgive their sin and will heal their land."

—2 Chronicles 7:14 (NIV)

"Trust in the Lord completely and do not rely on your own opinions. With all your heart rely on him to guide you, and he will lead you in every decision you make. Become intimate with him in whatever you do, and he will lead you wherever you go."

—Proverbs 3:5-6 (TPT)

"Your boast becomes a prophecy of a future failure. The higher you lift yourself up in pride the harder you'll fall in disgrace."

—Proverbs 16: 18 (TPT)

"Be willing to be made low before the Lord and he will exalt you!"

—James 4:10 (TPT)

SUBMIT YOURSELF FOR GOD'S PURPOSE

Humility, coupled with an obedient heart to surrender, unlocks the mysteries of your destiny. The moment you submit to the Lord, He will fill you with His Spirit. All it takes is your willingness to do so. Total surrender brings total infilling, and full submission brings complete fellowship. Your love of the Lord and Holy Spirit will burst you into a newly found joy. Thus, surrender and submission are necessary to move forward your spiritual discernment. This *mandates* you let go of your personal agenda to follow the Will and Ways of the Father. It calls for day-by-day repentance and loving the Holy Spirit to have moment-by-moment guidance. (**2 Corinthians 4:16**) Scripture calls for us to submit, to yield, to surrender to the Authority and Will of the Lord. It also means being subject to some conditions.

Those conditions include purity and humility of the heart. It means to have a relationship of reflection and revelation to learn your destiny and your purpose. *God will give you the green light clearing the way.* What he calls you to do, He will provide and equip you to accomplish, including but not limited to financing. This book is the perfect example. Last year I answered a call from Elijah's List to step into my destiny. I stepped into an opportunity with 1$ to embrace a platform for God's Destiny for Your Life. Long story short, I adopted in faith a platform from entrepreneur Steven K. to write a book. I did not know how I would finance this yet felt the Holy Spirit's Calling. You are reading the results of God providing all that is needed when we trust in Him. With trust in the Lord, you become His Micah Miracle in the making. (**Micah 6:8**) Micah summarizes the prophets' themes: act justly, love mercy and walk humbly (meaning with prudence) with your God. Daily, I intentionally submit myself to the purpose the Lord has for me. Never would I have imagined I could write anything. The Holy Spirit is the true author. Submit yourself and let God grow your tree for you.

God knows the purity of my heart as well as my desires. He also knows the wishes of the nature of my beloved. I seek for the Lord to encounter both my beloved and me. The Battle belongs to the Lord. The Blood of the Lamb with His Cleansing Grace makes it a Triune Blessing with Jesus. The shed blood of Yeshua *releases life* in you.

"So then, surrender to God. Stand up to the devil and resist him ad he will flee in agony. Move your heart closer and closer to God, and he will come even closer to you. But make sure you cleanse your life, you sinners and keep your heart pure and stop doubting."

—James 4:7-8 (TPT)

"Submit to God and be at peace with him; in this way prosperity will come to you. Accept instruction from his mouth and lay up his words in your heart."

—Job 22:21-22 (NIV)

"He has shown you a mortal what is good and what does the Lord require of you? To act justly and to love mercy and to walk humbly with your God."

—Micah 6:8 (NIV)

"We have become his poetry, a re-created people that will fulfill the destiny he has given each of us, we are joined to Jesus the Anointed One. Even before we were born, God planned in advance our destiny and the good works we would do to fulfill it."

—Ephesians 2:10 (TPT)

MY IDENTITY IS IN JESUS CHRIST We are called by the Lord to release trivial things that no longer matter. Yeshua asks me to stop looking for the greener pastures of others' pursuits and tend to my own from Him. He calls me to stay in my assigned lane. In that place, that lane, Jesus will bless my obedience and my humility. Now, more than ever in this time and season of the Lord I must seek His will and not the world's gold that glitters. Conversely, seek His Will to walk in faith, not by sight in our world today. I do this for my partner and all my family and my extended family whom I have chosen. The Lord is our fortress, our rock. (**Psalm 31:3**) Become a rock for your partner. Sometimes, I hear from those who seek me and my word about the times and season we now experience. I rest contently and remain unshaken. Remain unshaken by planting yourself in His Presence. (**1 John 4:4**) You could be the key to help someone unlock their prison. I must continue to seek the Lord's Wisdom and Will in all my mistakes and trials. They will be used for good. My future no longer depends on my past. God no longer remembers my past transgressions; then, why in the world would I keep them alive? (**Micah 7:18-19**) Instead, God uses my life for His Glory and His Good. *Whatever I bless for Him he will multiply for me*. This ties humility with trust. Trust to faith. Faith to substance that God is everything. The greater your trial, the greater will be your prayer blessing.

"Who is a God like you who pardons sin and forgives the transgression of the remnant of his inheritance? You do not stay angry forever but delight to show mercy. You will have compassion on us; you will tread our sins underfoot and hurl all our iniquities into the depts of the sea."

—Micah 7:18-19 (NIV)

"When you live a life of abandoned love, surrendered before the awe of God, here's what you'll experience: Abundant life. Continual protection, and complete satisfaction!"

—Proverbs 19:23 (TPT)

RETHINK YOUR GROCERY LIST PRAYERS. *Rejoice always! Pray without ceasing.* (**1 Thessalonians 5:16-18**) Pray over everything but not a grocery list of what you want God to do for you. I confess I remember once, praying for pearls. Clearly, the salvation of my partner and family has taken the place of things. The Holy Spirit will guide you in prayer. Prayer seeks not to change God's Will rather to reveal His Destiny and our purpose to best serve Him. Prayer calls to the Lord to hear your lament, your pain, or your troubled heart. We must first take that action in seeking God's mercy. Read the Psalms to understand laments. (**Psalm 5:1-3**) We all will need the Psalms. They help us move forward in our seeking. How about (**Psalm 126:5-6**)? I must seek for myself the answers for my Spiritual Union with God. I must let go of my tears to trust His Wisdom will reveal tender ways to bring Him into my marriage. I must wait on the Lord for His Timing.

"Rejoice always, pray continually, give thank in all circumstances; for this is God's will for you in Christ Jesus."

—1 Thessalonians 5:16-18 (NIV)

"Those who sow in tears will reap with songs of joy. He who goes out weeping, carrying seed to sow, will return with songs of joy, carrying sheaves with them."

—Psalm 126:5-6 (NIV)

God's timing will be your clue on shifting with humility. Could it be that our prayers reveal who we think we are, not what God says about us? As His vessel, you belong to Him. Make your body a sacred temple for the Holy Spirit's dwelling place. (**1 Corinthians 6:19-20**) Perhaps it is good to look at the time spent in prayer on the lesser things, things that don't matter. Think about what no longer matters in your life. Remember, as God's Bride, you are about the preparation daily to shift the lesser to embrace the Greater of the Lord for us. We should think about this as our life becomes devoted to Him. We want this to be a clear identity of devotion to the bridegroom. We can receive only what is given to us from heaven. (**James 1:22**) Sow good seeds to become a doer of the Word, not just a hearer of the Word.

Hear the Word to become the word. We just need to take what we have and do the best by letting God know our intention is pure. He will finish the rest by providing beyond our imagination! Become the word! Yes! This is turning over fallow ground. (**Hosea 10:12**) Through his unfailing love we are made whole by the Lord as we seek Him. So, this might encourage you to take your laments and turn them into praises allowing the Lord to bring His Will and Way to providing what you need, not what you want. My daughter Abby loves flowers. She loves arranging them and tending her potted plants and does so as a meditation. From trimming her fresh flowers to watering potted plants outdoors, she takes a mundane task and turning it into praise for the Lord.

Abby takes what she has and brings it to the Lord to allow God to provide what she is needing. Sunshine. Or take me in the Hallandale Symphony where I did what I could with what I had while God provided me that which I did not have. Courage to continue! Trust the Lord through faith in Him. Your prayers move the arm that moves the world. Be bold, stepping into fearless intercessory praying by faith. Walk in confidence to know your prayers matter. Walk in humility for strength to find contentment while contending.

"Let joy be your continual feast. Make your life a prayer. And in the midst of everything be always giving thanks, for this is God's perfect plan for you in Christ Jesus."

—1 Thessalonians 5:16-18 (TPT)

"If you bow low in God's awesome presence, he will eventually exalt you as you leave the timing in his hands."

—1 Peter 5:6 (TPT)

"...In relationship, each of you must wrap around yourself the apron of a humble servant because: God resists you when you are proud but multiplies grace and favor when you are humble."

—1 Peter 5:5 (TPT) *This says it!*

"Be a servant of the Lord. Always be an example for your spouse."

—2 Timothy 2:24 (NIV)

"Value others above yourself. Teach your spouse servanthood by example."

—John 13:14 (NIV)

"...the story of the Five Loaves and Two Small Fish...so they gathered and filled twelve baskets with the pieces of the five barley loaves left over by those who had eaten."

—John 6: 4-12 (NIV) *The Lord multiplied and provided what they could not do.*

TIME TO REVIEW AND REFLECT YOUR THOUGHTS.

Soon you have enough to create your own book!!!

- What new way are you called to show humility with your partner? Every small act of kindness will count here.

- How has your gift of being humble served the Lord? Are there changes with your beloved? A friend?

- Are you willing to train yourself to draw a line of resistance to your appetites or those your spouse desires?

- With this new awareness of humility, what things in the past now need to go? Just one thing.

- Do you carry pride in any area that needs to shift with your partner?

- Recall a time you walked away from trivial pursuits to honor the Lord. How did you feel about your choice? Did this humble you?

DECLARATION: Lord reveal a new level of humility for my path and plans to prosper my marriage and life. Help me, Lord, walk in humility, become teachable, and offer you an obedient heart.

REFLECT ON THE FOLLOWING AND WRITE YOUR THOUGHTS IN YOUR PRAYER JOURNAL:

- YOUR THOUGHTS TO JESUS

- IDEAS AND WORDS FROM JESUS

PRAYER: *Dear Lord, I come to you to examine my heart. May you find a contrite pure heart and one willing to repent when convicted by the Holy Spirit. Heavenly Father, I thank you for giving me, Yeshua, who died for me to take on my sin. Help me walk in humility as I obey your Will. Reveal my pride to me, Lord. Convict me, Holy Spirit. Lord, help me be humble as you have called me to be and repent for my misgivings. Thank you, Lord, for coming to heal my life, my beloved, and my household to find joy. Wrap your Presence around us, Lord Blanket us with your healing love. Allow my humility to soften the heart of my beloved, Lord. In Jesus Precious Name. Amen.*

Chapter 4
KINDNESS

Give Us this Day Our Daily Bread

SIFT AND SHIFT YOUR UNION WITH GENEROSITY—GOD'S WORDS ARE OUR DAILY BREAD

CHEF NOTE: I will never forget the day I purchased a bread maker. It was the kind you could take it to rise or let it finish with the baking. Well, I looked at that container and thought, how boring does that look. I researched and purchased a beautiful round "Cloche Baker" which would produce a professional and yummy looking round bread. Next, I put together a recipe with 7 grains to make it nutritious. Finally, after gathering it all together, I began my first bread taking it to the first rise, *then* moving to the Cloche for the second and final baking! Oh WOW!!! A mouth-watering winner! Literally, I entered my Seven Grain Super Bread in the local fair and won a first prize blue ribbon. After three years of winning, I decided it was time to stop entering and just enjoy the joy of baking it for others which became my signature gift of kindness! Kind of like Mother's Angel Food Cakes! Those were the amazing bread eating days gone by!

Jesus became our Daily Bread, and Living Word made flesh. He moves us to rise to new levels of personal commitment to become His Bride. He brought us the Father's Word with stories to convey a message. Parables to teach, which became His Great Gifts of kindness. He led the disciples to take communion with bread representing His Body and the wine representing a new Blood Covenant between God and His People. He became the Father's Plan for salvation, taking on our sins. The Daily Bread—what a magnificent phrase so layered with meaning.

Consider uncommon acts of generosity: "Giving gifts of food can bring great joy with your kindness." My husband and I lived on a boat for nearly ten years traveling from New England to South Florida and going up to Maine. My captain hubby talked me into doing a Charter Business. Oh, my goodness! We acquired a client who loved my Brownie Chocolate Cake. He was with us for a month, not onboard but on beck and call. We anchored off the house on a pond he had rented for a month that July on Martha's Vineyard. He discovered my chocolate cake! I made so many of them that month that I could do it by heart. My cake made his heart sing and probably became a waistline gift. Kindness came in the form of a cake. PS. It will make your heart sing too! See Di's Recipe Section, my friend.

It doesn't take much to show kindness which is truly the generosity of the Lord in the heart. So just imagine the generosity of our Father God giving us his Beloved Son, the Living Word, as our blueprint for life. Let us look at having this same generous spirit for our partners.

GOD GAVE US HIS ONLY BEGOTTEN SON.
(JOHN 3:16)

Jesus, our Living Word made flesh is God's most generous gifting to mankind. Yes, God in the person of Jesus became our salvation. Jesus, who is, was, and always will be, helped His Father form creation. God himself became His only begotten son as a Plan of Salvation for the fallen world. He became our sin. It remains the same today. Jesus came to bring the Father's Love and died for us to have Eternal Life. Jesus came to earth to the individual as a Son of Man and with His Divinity as the Son of God.

"Let us make mankind in our image, in our likeness so that they may rule over the sky, over the livestock and all the wild animals and over all the creatures that move on the ground."

—**Genesis 1:26** (NIV) Let **us** make mankind in **our** image, **our** likeness indicating the **"Trinity."**

"For God so loved the world that he gave his one and only Son, that whoever believes in him shall not perish but have eternal life."

—**John 3:16** (NIV)

"Except a man be born again he cannot see the Kingdom of God."

—**John 3:3** (NIV)

"Peace be with you! As the Father has sent me, I am sending you." And with that he breathed on them and said, "Receive the Holy Spirit. If you forgive anyone's sins their sins are forgiven; if you do not forgive them, they are not forgiven."

—John 20:21-22 (NIV)

FIX YOUR EYES ON JESUS THE WAY MAKER

As I grow spiritually, God's wisdom becomes a generous reality to share with my partner, with my children, and with my friendships. The Living Bible contains all I will ever need to know about living a life devoted to the Father. Keeping your eyes focused on life's problems will block your spiritual growth. Fixing your eyes on the Problem Solver, the Lord Jesus Christ will bless you with needed peace. Yeshua/Jesus is the answer. (**Proverbs 16:9**) It calls for you to trust Him as He Directs your steps.

Reluctantly, we put our condo up for sale in obedience to Jesus. After many conversations, the Lord kept saying do this. *Trusting the Lord*, it still took courage to make the phone call to the realtor. With hurricane season we took it off the market. Then, with God's perfect timing, one week after restoring it back to the listings, an offer came, and we accepted. This was Astonishing Joy at its finest! Honestly! Our next step then was where to go! Frustration set in after spending a great deal of time looking to move in the area, I stopped it all and placed my faith we would be shown our next steps. We waited, *in trust*, for the Lord to show us the way. We had two months to get this sorted out. Our realtor held an open house for several units that October in our building, including ours, and on the list was a rental two floors above us in the same stack. Oh Lord, could this be it! Indeed, just waiting for us was a newly remodeled, new place which offered a lovely view!

Arrangements were made. We moved in January of 2021 Within a week, all boxes were opened, and pictures hung. (**Psalm 28:7**) Indeed, Jesus gave me the supernatural strength to accomplish this. All Glory to him. We trusted completely to find the perfect place.

He prepared a place for us long before we knew we would need it. It is just thrilling to look back on the Lord's planning with His Perfect timing. When we *fix our eyes* and walk in trust, the Holy Spirit Power takes over. The Father's Spirit becomes the Living Word. Yeshua/Jesus is our most excellent example. He walked blamelessly, directed by the Holy Spirit to do only as the Father led. Yeshua is the only way to the Father God. (**John 14:6**) Fixing your eyes on Jesus will open His generosity to pour into your life. He knows what you need, what your partner needs, and when you need it. Don't be afraid of waiting, trusting, or changing because he will send His Holy Spirit to orchestrate everything!

Jesus answered "I am the way and the truth and the life. No one comes to the father except through me."

—John 14:6 (NIV)

CO-CREATE WITH HOLY SPIRIT POWER Being Born from Above brought incredible joy! (**2 Corinthians 1:3-4**) This put my marriage under the blanket of the comfort of the Holy Spirit so I might offer comfort to my partner. The Holy Spirit became my Guide, my Advocate, and my Helper. Holy Spirit has become my best friend! Daily, I tell the Holy Spirit how much I love Him. I feel His Presence with Holy Spirit rushes. He guides my prayers to the Father always. Dutch Sheets in his *"Give Him15 Daily Word"* speaks of growing into your ability to intercede and co-create with the Holy Spirit. Dutch says of using our gifts to pray for others. As believers Jesus is calling the

Church to step into bold action to pray for others. When Holy Spirit shows you someone, stop and pray. Intercessors for America provides another avenue for prayer! The Power of the Holy Spirit will direct you to what to do! We must be *willing and available* to do it! Be the one who would answer the Holy Spirit's call to stop and pray for something or someone. Whether through intercessory prayers, declarations, or sacrifices to atone for sin, our co-creating with the Spirit of the Father, we present the needs of humankind *to Heaven's Throne of Grace.* You are never more like Jesus than when you pray for one of His Children. We can also co-create to decree and declare the healing of the *earth, the land,* from the Father's Throne of Grace through prayers for the nations such as the Lord's Prayer. (**2 Chronicles:14**) Thy Kingdom come to Thy Will be done is a command. It causes us to be generous in our Spirit towards the human condition. Holy Spirit fills us when we seek our own repentance and pardon to cleanse us. This is the eternal gift of life. We are moved into greater faith through rebirth and renewal from the Father. (**Titus 3:5-7**) It is by grace we are saved through faith and not from ourselves. (**Ephesians 2:8**) It is a gift of God, not by work, so that no one can boast. Just imagine this understanding applied to our partners. Speak silently to the Holy Spirit Power to bless and renew our beloved partners. Every Holy Spirit moment will lift you higher into a place of humility and grace.

Step out of yourself to step into the Grace of the Holy Spirit Power. (**Romans 15:13**) Lay all your blessings on the altar of your heart to the Lord. It will prepare you to meet any challenges that follow to be generous with His Spirit. May this bring your heart hope and Astonishing Joy.

"But you will receive power when the Holy Spirit comes on you and you will be my witnesses in Jerusalem and in all Judea and Samaria and to the ends of the earth."

—Acts 1:8 (NIV)

"May the God of hope fill you with all joy and peace as you trust in him, so that you may overflow with hope by the power of the Holy Spirit."

—Romans 15:13 (NIV)

JESUS TELLS US TAKE AND MAKE TIME FOR ME.

What does this really mean? It means I am called to draw the line of resistance to things pulling me away from Yeshua. After reading the story of Daniel along with Hananiah, Mishael, and Azariah, all of which are better known by the Babylonia names: Belteshazzar, Shadrach, Meshach, and Abednego, resistance comes alive! Their first line of resistance to the King came through food. (**Daniel 1:8**) Permission was granted to prove their diet of vegetables and water proved the superior diet too rich foods and wine. *They "drew the line of resistance."* Daniel surrendered his life to the Lord. Like Jesus with the Father, he did not make a move without confirmation from the Father. So, it wasn't surprising that certain activities no longer held an appeal for me. More importantly, I pondered how best to create a Sacred Time and Space with my family dynamics in play. This was the beginning of my personal surrender to Messiah. Going to bed early was a simple solution that blessed me with the ability to rise early for quiet and necessary time without interruption.

My daily habits shifted. In the early quiet hours, I discovered the deepest hunger for the Living Word of God. With the added value of setting up my Sacred Space and Sacred Time, I began to "Draw the Line of Resistance," shifting all my Daily habits. My new daily disciplines serve me best by creating a mindset that moves my mind to expect all good. I give my first fruits to the Lord. Early morning hours are my most productive, and I hear from the Holy Spirit in the quiet. It makes such a difference for the day. *Quiet moments evolved into a quieted soul.* My advice: remain steadfast in creating time for the Lord. Next, I stopped the news and devoted more time to reading. My exercise routine was refined. Although you feel cut off from the world's activity, your soul treasures the eternal food that no one can take away. Heaven will bless your quiet time. The Lord will *stretch out* your time. (**Colossians 4:5-6**) My marriage atmosphere vastly improved because of my faith and perseverance in creating new times for myself, resulting in a new level of peace to my soul. This helped me become a vessel of joy. It brings salt and light to my marriage. My worship time establishes the frequency for the day, increasing my desire to offer acts of kindness. It helps me set my mind for the day with my beloved to walk in obedience, humility, and generosity of my spirit. The more centered I am, the more confidence I have in my partner. The more centered I am, the more I say no to disruptions of my precious time.

MAKING YES YOUR YES AND NO YOUR NO

When I began to seek answers in the Word, it meant I was choosing the Wisdom of God over the knowledge of man. I made severe shifts in my reading materials, reading only books filled with encouragement in place of fiction that often filled the mind improperly. I dropped out of a book club after several selected books just did not meet my criteria. Years ago, I stopped reading and buying fashion magazines. I no longer watch the TV news. I am cautious about which movies I would go to see. My desires for them ceased primarily because of content as well as the use of my time. Thank the Lord we are seeing a rise in Kingdom Based films. I love watching Christian Cinema featuring biblical figures on my computer. This Hollywood shift will take over the Mountain of Entertainment. Praise God! Say yes and amen to being steadfast and disciplined to make a difference.

Add to the Kingdom with all your personal choices. Fasting regularly adds to my shift to the Kingdom. Now, I regard Daniels's approach to eating—fruits vegetables. The Book of Daniel will bless you. I started watching my food intake. As a part of my Youthful Aging Lifestyle concept, I encourage everyone to carefully consider their body temple. Intermittent fasting cleanses my body as well as my mind and soul. (**1 Corinthians 6:19-20**) My personal health and vitality are blessed with my good habits. Prayer and fasting produced a powerful way to strengthen devotion, seek God's guidance, express repentance to humble me, and return to the Lord. Daniel turned to the Lord for the answer in his training in Babylon. (**Daniel 1:17**) You can be a Daniel for your partner.

"But Daniel resolved not to defile himself with the royal food and wine, and he asked the chief official for permission not to defile himself this way."

—Daniel 1:8 (NIV)

"I turned to the Lord God and pleaded with him in prayer and petition, in fasting and in sackcloth and ashes."

—Daniel 9:3 (NIV)

BEING IN A HURRY IS NOT OF GOD.

Your Time is Your Life. Dr. Joseph Peck, known as the Time Doctor, encourages a new and fresh approach to using your time. I highly recommend His book and webinar: *I Was Busy Now I'm Not*, especially with regards to time margins. Schedule time margins to allow the Holy Spirit to make departures and detours in your day. Scheduling downtime is a yes to being blessed. Slowing down was not easy in the beginning nor was being on time. These two bad habits were flaws in my character. After disappointing my partner before we were married, I said no more. Ever notice how irritated you are when someone isn't on time? I began to realign my priorities. I remember years ago my dear friend waited on me for in a restaurant for lunch. She felt insulted about my being late as her time was a valuable as mine. After that incident, I put into place time margins. These margins are now used for Holy Spirit moments of interruption. Be sure to look at this for yourself. Dr. Peck is right. Time is your life. Use it wisely.

What matters most needs to be done first. Important things come first. Seek the Lord first. When we have time margins for the Lord to operate in our lives, then time stretches itself out. One more thing. Jesus never did hurry. Dr. Peck says we must ruthlessly eliminate hurry. His book is such a blessing. He helps you understand the difference between time wasted and time redeemed.

"So above all instantly seek God's kingdom and his righteousness then all these less important things will be give to your abundantly."

—Matthew 6:33 (TPT)

"Set your minds on things above not on earthly things."

—Colossians 3:2 (NIV)

DAILY SCRIPTURE / DAILY DISCIPLINES / DAILY KINDNESS TO MYSELF.

Redeemed time is eternal. I shifted my waking hours. Apart from loving the early morning hours, I discovered a whole new world of quiet called the "Golden Hours" from 5–8 a,m. I awaken often at 3 a.m. and rise at 4 a.m. to read the Living Word and give praise and glory to the Lord. Suddenly, I had great peace in my soul, making time for the *things of God.* Of course, these golden hours are so ideal for working on assignments from God. It allows me to ruthlessly eliminate hurry later in the day. So much more is accomplished vs. hit the floor running style of life. Now I organize my life to offer my time margins for Holy Spirit to have me take actions I otherwise might have missed. *I began to understand how time reflects my life.* I stopped wasting time on trivial matters. Now, I accomplish so much more as God stretches out my time on that which serves Him with redeemed time. You see, wasted time is lost. Sacred Time is eternal and forever. It adds to your bank account in heaven. Giving your time becomes your greatest gift to God.

My bible study time is my daily bread. This makes my heart sing!!! Now, my time matters. The promises of the Lord come to life for me, witnessing them in real-time. Again, there is everything I need to live under the wings of the Lord. The generosity of the Father comes to us as a *living word* and our Daily Bread. We are fed through His Word with time to find the answers. The bible helps me answer questions and have discussions in a new and fresh way in my marriage. As Priestess and Kings seated in heavenly places, we must also speak from this place.

(**Ephesians 2:6**) Command from this place. Begin to think about how you can alter your life from this place. It all begins with time and how you use it. (**Mark 13:32**) We must remain alert for the time of the Lord's return. We do not know the hour or the day. Be on guard! Be Alert.

"And God raised us up with Christ and seated us with him in the heavenly realms in Christ Jesus."

—Ephesians 2:6 (NIV)

"There is a time for everything. A season for every activity under the heavens."

—Ecclesiastes 3:1 (NIV)

"Truth's shining light guides me in my choices and decisions; the revelation of your Word makes my pathway clear."

—Psalm 119:105 (TPT)

"I sought the Lord and he answered me; He delivered me from All my fears."

—Psalm 34:4 (NIV)

"Our lives are a Christ-Like Fragrance rising up to God."

—2 Corinthians 2:15 (NIV)

"We have become the unmistakable aroma of the victory of the Anointed One to God."

—2 Corinthians 2:15 (TPT)

"The Lord is not slow in keeping his promise as some understand slowness. Instead he is patient with you not wanting anyone to perish, but for everyone come to repentance."

—2 Peter 3:9 (NIV)

GIVING AND RECEIVING CREATES GENEROSITY WITH YOUR TREASURES.

Have you ever wondered about tithing? Tithing in the Kingdom is *"given"* to be coming from a place of *Honoring God*. We don't tithe to get blessed; we tithe because we are blessed. It is not like paying an electric bill. (**Malachi 3:10**) This scripture is used in most churches today which addresses the Levitical Priesthood of Israel where tithing was simply payment for priestly service rendered. Dr Myles tells us tithing under the Order of Melchizedek is "giving of a royal endowment of honor" to the "Crown King." We tithe to advance the Kingdom, not manipulate our spiritual leaders to give "priestly services" we think we deserve. Finally, some perceive and labor under the notion tithing is to get a financial return. Dr. Myles in his book *Tithe$ of Honor* teaches to stop tithing for money! Some withhold tithes which robs them of a Spiritual Blessing. Our tithe attests to God's Blessings we already have in our lives. We can then sow offerings into the work of the Kingdom.

One of the greatest benefits for tithing is God's interception of the enemy for you. *Tithing becomes a protection for your money against the demonic powers and technologies that hate to see Christians succeeding.* Tithing in the Kingdom's New Creation is bringing down Heaven with your Honor to the Father. It becomes a sign you have surrendered your heart to the Father. It has to do with shifting your mindset to receive the blessings of the Father abundantly!!! Surrender to the Father and He will bless you *always* with everything you need including money on which you tithe. You will be delighted to learn through *The Order of Melchizedek* the principle of wealth transfer comes from the Father's desire to bless each of us. (**Hebrews 7—please read.**) This blessing comes in the form of ideas the Lord places in those who walk in Kingdom dedicating and surrendering to the Father God. You will also learn the importance of the Bread and Wine of Communion Abraham was given. It was a covenant between Abraham and God with the promise of protection making him the Father of all the Nations. I strongly suggest you purchase Dr. Myles book *The Order of Melchizedek* and *Tithe$ of Honor*. Consider enrolling in the Empower 2000 *Order of Melchizedek Teaching*. He also covers in depth the need for a Spiritual Altar in your life.

God's Blessings come through belief backed with *faith*. (**Galations 3**) Read Galatians 3 to understand miracles come from Faith, not works of the Law. (**V3**) Invest now into understand how God will favor each of us with ideas to bring us Kingdom Wealth for you then to tithe back to the Father. (**Mark 11:23-24**) Have faith in God. The Father wants to pour out heaven's blessings over each of us. New ideas given requires encouragement to obey and pursue. It is through your obedience that the Holy Spirit will make the way clear. The Teachings of Apostle Myles will transform your understating of returning to God that what he has given to you. (**Isaiah 51:1-3**) Abraham (Abram) encountered Melchizedek in the Valley of the Kings after achieving great victory over the enemy Kings. His Spiritual Encounter with Melchizedek shifted him supernaturally into the Kingdom Priesthood through taking Kingdom Based Communion with Him which delivered him from the enemy. He then gave his first tenth tithe from these spoils to Melchizedek (**Genesis 14:18**) Abraham was in awe and reverence of Melchizedek. The complete surrender of Abraham to God was with unwavering belief and faith he was established in God's Kingdom and able to *say no to the devices of the King of Sodom*. Abraham gave back all the remaining spoils to be able to say the King of Sodom never made his rich. Every idea from the Father is intended to bless His Kingdom Purposes. This is your calling to step into this Kingdom under the authority of the Jesus, His Son, and the High Priest of the Order of Melchizedek. Through this teaching you will understand the need to embrace the Kingdom of Heaven, giving God all the Glory. Realize then that "offerings multiply" to come back to you for the purpose of the expansion of the Kingdom of Heaven. (**Proverbs 3:9-10**) The gift you give sows into someone or something as an offering from your hand to multiply it. This does not apply to lifestyle purposes but for God's Kingdom expansion. There is no multiplication in buying and selling. Only *sowing* multiplies. (**Matthew 6:20-21**) Consult with the Lord on offerings you can make. Be guided in this to multiply the balance in your Treasures in Heaven Account. I encourage you to embrace the Order of Melchizedek Teachings They will bless your partner and family.

"But store up for yourselves treasure in heaven, where moths and vermin do not destroy and where thieves do not break in and steal. For where your treasure is, there your heart will be also."

—Matthew 6:13 (NIV)

This applies to the offerings you make to ministries, families, partners, and all that God presents to you for just this opportunity of multiplication. **You** are God's vessel for the Spirit of giving. God multiplies the Kingdom through your gifts and talents. *Take a moment now and read (**2 Corinthians 9:6-15**) to see how generosity is connected to your worth.* Find ways to become a cheerful giver in whatever you do you are doing for the Lord. Ideas might include helping a neighbor, adopt a widow, carry snacks or grocery cards for the homeless or food pantries. Through your service, you are giving thanksgiving to the Father. My Ft. Lauderdale Woman's Club offers six ways to serve the community. I call it one-stop shopping for volunteering!!! You cannot receive what you do not provide. Your outflow determines your inflow. You are blessed to be a blessing.

"Each of you should give what you have decided in your heart to give not reluctantly or under compulsion for God loves a cheerful giver. And God is able to bless you abundantly so that in all things at all time having all that you need you will abound in every good work."

—2 Corinthians 9:7-8 (NIV)

"Not that I desire your gifts: what I desire is that more be credited to your account."

—Philippians 4:17 (NIV) Paul is saying thank you for the gifts and more importantly, you are growing the size of your (Treasures in Heaven) account. He even goes on saying *"And God will meet all your needs according to the riches of his glory in Jesus Christ."*

"Ship your grain across the sea; after many days you may receive a return."

—Ecclesiastes 11:1 (NIV)

Another version:

"Give generously. For your gifts will return to you later."

—Ecclesiastes 11:1 (TLB)

ADORN YOURSELF WITH INNER BEAUTY.

Unbelievers are like stray sheep. They are being called to return to the Shepherd and Overseer of their soul. (**1Peter 2:25,3**) This merits your study, "Wives, in the same way, submit yourselves to our own husband so if any of them do not believe the word they may be won over without words by the *behavior of their wives* when they see the purity and reverence of your lives." It goes on to say, let your inner beauty shine the Christ Light on our beloveds. It will be that inner beauty, the unfading beauty of a gentle and quiet spirit so worthy in God's Sight. The holy women of the biblical past put their hope in God to adorn themselves. Through this humility comes compassion and a deep understanding of ministering with words to heal, not destroy. Our calling blesses, not tears down. Our experience comes from above, not below. Our inner beauty becomes the unfading beauty of a gentle and quiet spirit that brings worth to God's sight and His Living Word to their hearts.

"You were like sheep that continually wandered away, but now you have returned to the true Shepherd of your lives—the kind Guardian who lovingly watches over your souls."

—1 Peter 2:25 (TPT)

BRINGING THE WORD TO MY PARTNER

Slowly, with kindness, I bring forth my daily devotions to my beloved. This includes my prayers for people, prayers before meals, and often prayers before bed to heal the atmosphere. I walk out what the Holy Spirit shows me.

Slowly and tenderly, my beloved acknowledged me helping others in prayer along with acts of kindness. (**Proverbs 11:25**) These are small things that make a huge difference in your beloved's salvation and your marriage. It just means the generosity of the Father imparted to the Son now imparted for each of us to pass along to the Body of Christ. (**Psalm 63:7**) I will sing to you Lord in the shadow of your wing because you are upholding my partner and me with your right hand.

JOURNAL FOR THE JOY—REVIEW AND REFLECTION.

Are you feeling any shifts at this midway point?

- What new and fruitful ways have come to express your kindness to your partner? Name one or create one.

- Do you have a daily prayer time to hear from the Lord and to read his Living Word? This is generosity to yourself.

- Find a scripture that becomes your anchor with the Lord. Soak in it to bring the gift of generosity alive in your soul.

- Do you have devotions with your beloved? Do you pray before meals? Do your children pray before bed? Pray with them.

- Find new ways to add spiritual value to your family life. Think about this.

- What one thing can shift you today to deepen your relationship with the Lord? Deepen your nurturing of your relationship with your partner? What new kindness can you offer to yourself?

DECLARATION: Today I begin a new life in the Lord. Today I shed my past sufferings and failures to master my emotions.

REFLECT ON THE FOLLOWING AND WRITE YOUR THOUGHTS IN YOUR PRAYER JOURNAL:

- YOUR WORDS TO JESUS

- IDEAS AND WORDS FROM JESUS

PRAYER: *Lord, you have blessed me so generously with gifts and fruits from the Holy Spirit. Lord, I lean on the promise of your Word as I repent for any actions that have taken me off my path, Lord. I step into a new spiritual authority with the Holy Spirit, lifting my abilities to match my destiny plans you have created for me. Lord, I pray to hunt with words that prosper and bear fruit, Lord, with my kindness. Let my lips speak only that which pleases you, Lord, to my beloved partner. Help me to walk in your countenance to bring the image of you to my family and especially my beloved partner Lord through me. Thank you, Lord, for your everlasting arms of Love. In Jesus Precious Name, AMEN.*

Chapter 5

COURAGE

Forgive My Trespasses as I Forgive Those Who Trespass Against Me

SIFT AND SHIFT YOUR UNION WITH FORGIVENESS…A LIFESTYLE OF FORGIVENESS

CHEF NOTE: My mother. Oh, how I admire her more than ever today. You know dad went to work every morning early with a lunchbox. She was in the kitchen first thing for Dad's lunch. She always had my tea ready with milk when I came home from high school at noon. I just took it for granted then. Looking back, it seemed she was always cooking something. Mondays were laundry days. If it was bad weather things were strung in the kitchen. Oh, and she made her own laundry soap for a wringer machine that sat on the back mud room. The kitchen, for sure, was her domain. The kitchen is my power room as well! My desk faces the windows and behind me is the stove! Mom had a desk in her kitchen! Her white table by the sink held her notes and lists. So, that's where my listing making skills started!!! She used envelopes from mail to make her grocery lists and reminders of things. She was always cooking up something for others as well. I remember a moment as if it were yesterday. Mom had made a pie for a family that had a death. She was so kind to people. I learned from her. Her pies spoke louder than her words could say. It came up at the dinner table (yes, we sat down at the table every night for dinner together) about the pie. I think my dad felt left out or something because he said, what about *our pie*. I was crushed for my mother. Silence followed. Mother responded with such humility. The thing I remember, though, was how sorry my dad was for his words. I think it was the first time I witnessed forgiveness between them, all over a pie. That moment was a life lesson for me. Sometimes the most challenging thing is to be sorry and say, please forgive me.

Jesus reminds us, unless we forgive, we will not be forgiven by the Father

I have come to view forgiveness as non-negotiable. It takes courage to forgive. When I walk with the (**Hebrews 1:3**) Light of the Lord, I must walk in forgiveness. It is crucial to take forgiveness very seriously because it is necessary for having eternal life. To be forgiven by the Father God, the Just and Righteous Judge, you must walk in forgiveness. These verses say it all:

"For if you forgive men when they sin against you, your heavenly Father will also forgive you. But if you do not forgive men their sins your Father will not forgive your sins."

—Matthew 6:9-15 (NIV)

"Refuse to be a critic full of bias toward others, and you will not be judged."

—Matthew 7:1 (TPT)

FORGIVE MYSELF

Forgiveness must begin from my heart. I must first start with me. This means I need to release guilt to not feel shame. This truth needs to be remembered over and over when you forgive yourself. To accept the *Total Forgiveness* from the Father with forgiving others and forgiving myself means I must let go and let God. Again, forgiveness needs to be non-negotiable. We do not have to approve of a person who has wronged us or spend time with the person, yet we must seek to forgive them. It is through the shed blood of Yeshua, who died for our sins, that makes this possible. I look at myself in the mirror to remind myself God has forgiven me. It has gone to the sea of forgetfulness. (**Micah 7:19**) The longer I hang on to a wound, the deeper it gets. It calls for great humility to release a grudge or even nurse a hurt as God wants you to lay it all aside. I must become *unoffendable*. (**1 Corinthians 13:5**) Only through the Father can the wound heal completely. There is no need to keep rehearsing and allow anyone to live rent-free in our minds, which keeps them alive in our souls. What you focus on will expand, so guard your thoughts. (**Proverbs 4:23**) Time blesses us. Time heals and allows discovery of the blessings and gifts that come through the forgiveness of wrongdoings. I highly recommend RT Kendall's *Total Forgiveness* to grasp the fullness that comes from forgiving, especially in areas of rejection.

Rejection isn't the end; it is the beginning. Hope and excitement filled me as I headed off to attend Kansas State University in the fall of 1960 for Sorority Rush Week before the fall semester. You must remember my hometown is tiny and an unknown Kansas town. Attending the gatherings and meetings with the members of all the groups gave me insight into each house as well as myself. Daily, you were to narrow your choices down as the houses did the same things. In a perfect world, your choice would be their choice as well. It came the last day. Carefully, I studied the various groups and watched how I felt about them. However, when it came time to get it to the line to receive the invitation for membership, I was handed a note that said, *Panhellenic regrets* to inform you there are no invitations. This happened to the three of us. Amid screaming girls, I straightened myself and said, thank you, and walked away to find the nearest phone. Even yet today, I come near to tears just recalling the whole event. No such thing as a cell phone in 1960. I called home and asked mom and dad to come a get me. This was the most profound rejection in my young life. I acted as if no big deal, but honestly, it was a deep, deep wound. With spiritual wisdom, I was finally able to see God was taking care of me. His plan was to keep me from a path that didn't fit my destiny. *Listen to me,* turn that feeling into joy because you were prevented from moving forward. Regardless of the rejection, be blessed you were stopped.

God had other plans for me. I was blessed in the Spring of my freshman year a new sorority house was established on campus. I went for it and found my inner circle of life-long friends on my terms. Spiritually, I now see Holy Spirit guided me to what was to be connections that shifted my life. I could not have known this at the time. I share this to spare you should rejection come into your life and likely it will. Ask the Holy Spirit to show it to you from a higher and favored perspective to attain release, peace, and freedom. (**2 Corinthians 3:17**) Most of all, forgive yourself for thinking you are less than you are. Forgiveness allows us to refine our strength with courage.

FORGIVE MY PARTNER

It takes courage to forgive your beloved. It takes discernment to stop keeping a long list of records. It takes strength to silently ignore and return to your task. (**Colossians 3:13**) A secret key to understanding conflicts involves the enemy who loves to get to us through our partners or family members. Healing yourself first allows you to support the healing God will do *through you and your heart*. All forgiveness begins in the heart. Soon and in a while, those triggers from your partner will cease. Hallelujah! Sometimes the minor comments create the largest waves of inner response. *When forgiveness becomes a mantra, then the incident can be viewed with a fresh understanding.* Immediately, I forgive to again recall the enemy loves to steal and destroy. (**John 10:10**) It could be a stronghold that needs to have its power broken bound, destroyed, and delivered. It can be a difficult situation. This issue can cause much stress for the believer. Never miss an opportunity to stop and bless your beloved. Silently, the Lord gives you many opportunities to express His Love to each of your family members. Train the mind to keep on the outlook for the thief who loves to cause a divided house. Understand the nature of Satan, and you will conquer your giants. God's people are so blessed because God not only forgives, and He also forgets! He is a God of Forgetfulness into the sea of forgetfulness.

"You will again have compassion on us; you will tread our sins underfoot and hurl all our iniquities into the depths of the sea."

—Micah 7:19 (NIV)

"Love is patient Love is kind. It does not envy, it does not boast, it is not proud It does not dishonor others. It is not self-seeking. It is not easily angered, it keeps no record of wrongs."

—1 Corinthians 13:4-5 (NIV)

"All this is from God who reconciled us to himself through Christ and gave us the ministry of reconciliation; that God was reconciling the world to himself in Christ not counting people's sins against them."

—2 Corinthians 5:18-19 (NIV) God has given us this ministry of restoring relationships.

The Blood of the Lamb cleanses me and forgives me from past wrongdoings. He was crucified to offer Himself as a Lamb of God with His Body and the Spiritually Pure DNA of His Blood. As God's Covenant to His People, this Shed Blood offers cleansing and eternal redemption. The Father so loved the world he gave His only begotten Son Jesus as a Plan for Salvation. (**John 3:16**) Being unequally yoked suddenly released in me a heavy heart. I could not put it aside any longer. Now, in writing this message I see God using my choices to serve the Kingdom through my story. My forgiveness moved into a deepening trust in my walk with the Lord. His Blood of the Lamb cleansed my soul and healed me with this Promise for Eternal Life. It was not the end but a beginning of my destiny plan. Your situation can be lifted as you step into a new life with new authority. You are called to serve the Living God with a freshly examined heart filled with His Peace and Joy. This means you are making yourself *willing and available* for the Lord. The Body and the Blood of Christ becomes your healing power. Communion offers the release of guilt or shame through repentance. (**Acts 3:19**) Daily, seek intimacy with Christ. Daily, I literally put on the Armor of God as my healing protection. (**Ephesians 6:10-17**)

To protect my thinking, my lips to guard my speaking, and my heart to make right knowing, I walk by faith with two final prayers: **The 23rd Psalm** and the **Psalm 91** Prayer of Protection. I especially love the safety and security of the TPT version of the Psalm 91. It sets in place my readiness to meet the day's challenges. I feel the Lord's Blessed Assurance with Him as my Rear Guard. (**Isaiah 58:8**) You are redeemed by the Precious Blood of Christ, a lamb without blemish or defect. This restores and renews my belief no harm can come to me or mine. This helps me prevent offense from coming into my heart. Reset now your entire lives in devotion to the Lord God's forgiveness with repentance and His Precious Blood of the Lamb Cleansing. These prayers will protect the soil of your heart to receive fresh mercies from the Lord.

WITH REPENTANCE COMES GOD'S FRESH MERCIES AND FORGIVENESS

Forgiveness from the Father brings me to a place of being thankful for His Fresh Mercy morning after morning. (**Lamentations 3:23**) We receive fresh mercy through God's Faithfulness. I love the hymn, *Great is Thy Faithfulness*. Make your focus on your blessings, not your problems. Once you feel forgiveness, move on. No need to keep asking because God has already forgotten and sent it to the Sea of Forgetfulness. The hope of forgiveness arrives fresh every morning, followed by gratitude every night for these gifts of His Mercy. Thank you, Father, for the hope that forgiveness brings! Oh hope, you bring us such joy. Hope moves us into faith. Ask yourself, where would you be without hope? Hope becomes your anchor to remain on solid ground during the storm. (**Hebrews 6:19**) It is the lynchpin of faith. Hope literally heals the soul. These three, mercies, forgiveness, and hope, help us to reset our daily lives. Should you encounter a conflict with your partner, reconcile before bedtime with forgiveness. *To avoid regrets, reconcile quickly. Can you forgive me?* This helps to prevent the root of bitterness from setting in. It stops the mental reliving of an event. This restores peace. Be the first one to do so. Then there is age-old wisdom: Never go to bed angry. (**2 Corinthians 5:19**) Reconcile to rest in peace Then yes, get up the next morning afresh. You have fresh forgiveness every morning. Hallelujah! New forgiveness lavishes God's Favor over you.

"Because of the Lord's great love we are not consumed, for his compassions never fail. They are new every morning; great is your faithfulness."

—Lamentations 3:22-23 (NIV)

"Great is Thy Faithfulness," Refrain: Great is they faithfulness! Great is they Faithfulness! Morning by morning new mercies I see; all I have needed they hand hath provided; great is they faithfulness, Lord unto me!

—United Methodist Hymnal (page 140)

"Hear my voice, O God! Answer this prayer and hear my plea for mercy. Lord, if you measured us and marked us with our sins who would ever have their prayers answered? But your forgiving love is what makes you so wonderful! No wonder you are loved ad worshiped!"

—Psalm 130:2-4 (TPT)

"We have hope as an anchor for the soul, firm and secure. It enters the inner sanctuary behind the curtain where our forerunner, where Jesus has entered on our behalf. He has become a high priest forever in the order of Melchizedek."

—Hebrews 6:19-20 (NIV)

"For as high as the heavens are above the earth, so great is his love for those who fear him; as far as the east is from the west so far has he removed our transgressions from us."

—Psalm 103:11-12 (NIV)

ATTRACTING THE FAVOR OF GOD WITH DAILY REPENTANCE

God's Favor for forgiveness comes when walking in obedience and humility. Forgiveness calls for a humble heart to deal with repentance for regrets. As I have mentioned earlier, these feelings of sadness for certain things can live rent-free in your mind. It is time to let them go. Remember, RT Kendall's book *Total Forgiveness*, mentioned earlier, relates the following, which can be astonishing to grasp: Never go to a person and say to them, "I forgive you." This will be counterproductive every time unless the person seeks to be forgiven. In reality, nine times out of ten, most do not feel they have even done anything wrong in attempting to forgive. It is up to me to forgive them from *my heart*—and then keep quiet about it and let it go. Yes, it all comes from the heart. We are asking the Lord God to forgive our sins and wrongdoings. Repentance reveals a contrite heart filled with humility to make a wrong right. We turn away. (**2 Chronicles 7:14**) This is so important, yet many times hard to do. It takes courage to let go and release. However, this action brings freedom to marriage. No more long repeated list of wrongs. Remember, my friend, humility coupled with forgiveness provides you with one of God's most excellent healing tools delivered by the Holy Spirit Power.

"If my people, who are called by my name, will humble themselves and pray and seek my face and turn from their wicked ways, then I will hear from heaven, and I will forgive their sin and will heal their land."

—2 Chronicles 7:14 (NIV)

When the Holy Spirit brings on conviction, then you know what to do. You can just feel it happen by stepping off a Godly Path. *Pause immediately to acknowledge and obey Holy Spirit for a release with repentance and turning away.* Carrying a burden of sin distorts the peace of the mind, body, and soul. I know because I did just this from 2012 to 2019, seven profound years of listening to the lies of the darkness. I was blinded to the point of losing all reason. Beware of Satan's snakes in money bags of gold. Misery on many levels is backed by the feeling of unworthiness. Shame. Arrogance coupled with pride is just where the enemy loves us to be. Finally, it ended. It died literally one day, and exposure flooded my soul. Repentance flooded my soul. The Lord produced a *"Suddenly."* Remember, *rend the heart with pioneer joy* and God's gracious Love. **(Joel 2:13)** Such regret mixed with joyous relief. What might you be hanging on to which stems from a pure lie? It happens, and it needs to be released, my friend. Release of it brings new freedom. **(Galatians 5:1)** Set yourself free. Thus, repentance expands your authority. Repent daily. Discipline with the small things will get you such favor in the more important things. Make sure in all you are doing to seek the *Favor of God* by showing Him your contrite heart. Ask for His Favor when you are doing everything. Seek it before an important call. Seek Him when you are dealing with your partner. Attracting the Favor of God begins with the obedience to forgive. Favor releases the fuel you need to grow into the Holy Spirit's Power. Hearing from the Holy Spirit starts with listening.

"If we boast that we have no sin, we're only fooling ourselves and are strangers to the truth. But if we freely admit our sins when his light uncovers them, he will be faithful to forgive us every time. God is just to forgive us our sins because of Christ, and he will continue to cleanse us from all unrighteousness."

—1 John 1:8-9 (TPT)

"And Jesus grew in wisdom and stature, and in favor with God and man."

—Luke 2:52 (NIV)

ACTIVELY LISTEN TO SEEK FORGIVENESS

Oh, to be quick to listen and slow to speak!!! James has it right. **James 1:19** encourages us to take time to listen. I mean time without any of your personal agenda to listen to your beloved. Seek out the wounded places of their past. It will dissolve the hardness that may have formed in their heart. Bring compassion to your listening. Bring them wisdom about the need to forgive and why. Forgiveness helps them understand the Lord seeks to forgive those who forgive others for offenses. Radical listening opens the hidden places to align in more profound ways. Listening can be a tuning fork for the heart. Your frequency can shift something inside. Remember, sifting is the separation of something. Sift and shift. This can be a beautiful heart-to-heart moment. Over dinner at day's end marks my favorite time to seek out my beloved. It can become a peaceful Holy Presence moment. I have discovered it brings a newfound intimacy to our marriage that watching tv doesn't allow. Turn off the news and make time for your beloved to speak, however long it takes for them to open heart. Forgiveness often comes along with a sense of peace and harmony. This calls for real work to help them find a true and deep release. *Actively listen to your partner.* This can lead to releasing a beautiful atmosphere of restoration and new ways to deepen your love for each other. This can open the door of the heart for the Lord's salvation.

PEACE COMES TO THE HEART WITH FORGIVENESS

The Lord wants His Children to have peace in their souls. When I was a little girl, caring for gardens required a great deal of time. Endless cucumbers and tomatoes occupied Dad while Mom cared for her flowers. Her peonies were my favorite. I was assigned the Strawberry Patch to tend and weed. I found great peace in weeding and making my garden shine and of course sampling as I weeded! Now, looking back I realize it was a life lesson. Weeds are thoughts that need to be brought into harmony with the Kingdom. Partners in unity will provide harmony for their children. Unbelief can disrupt this harmony and will require discernment. For example, issues with the partner's natural father may cause difficulty trusting the Father in Heaven. Greg Gunn offers a great solution. His mission to awaken families to greater harmony is spelled out in his book *Family ID*. He offers five core values essential for family unity. It all begins with a *Vision for the Family.* (**Proverbs 29:18**) *Where there is no vision people perish.* Children growing up under a family vision will be more grounded in the Lord for their future mates, lives, and destinies. Consider this book for your family's walk with the Lord.

Families thrive with a vision to embrace all the generations to follow. Family prayer becomes an essential key. This is where anointed prayers for healing love with forgiveness will bring peace. Only the love of the affectionate Father God can heal. His Son was sent to heal the brokenhearted. **(Isaiah 61:1)** and set the captives free. **(Luke 4:18)** Forgiveness offers freedom from grief and peace in your soul. **(Romans 15:13)** Discord robs you of peace. *Peace* comes from your heart. *Peace* in your soul shifts an atmosphere. *Peace* in your face/eyes becomes the softest and more precious gift of God. *Peace* will woo your lover. *Peace* in your heart allows for healing to come to your partner. Reconcile quickly for Your Inner Peace. This means peace with your partner and your family, friends, and especially your God. My goodness, every son and daughter need the Father's Peace as well. It is never too late to address the need for your family to have a vision.

"The Spirit of the Sovereign Lord is on me, because the Lord has anointed me to proclaim good news to the poor. He has sent me to bind up the brokenhearted, to proclaim freedom for the captives and release from darkness for the prisoners."

—Isaiah 61:1 (NIV)

"...then God's wonderful peace that transcends human understanding will guard your heart and mind through Jesus Christ."

—Philippians 4:7 (TPT)

"And I find that the strength of Christ's explosive power infuses me to conquer every difficulty."

—Philippians 4:13 (TPT)

CHILDREN WILL MODEL YOUR HARMONY AND PEACE

Your personal harmony will silently teach your child. A family vision as above mentioned will start children off on the way they should go. Parents are to lead their children to know the Lord. (**Proverbs 22:6**) Become a good teacher for your children by modeling forgiveness with your partner and teaching them to do the same with their friends. Your marriage becomes the example for your child to follow. We become the example. *Our intentions can root them* in Christ for a lifetime. Your forgiveness will create memories for them to recall in adulthood. Model repentance. Modeling becomes a good example worth a thousand words. May Day in my tiny Kansas town meant the lilacs were blooming along with Iris and Tulips. Mom would help be make construction cones to fill them with candy at the bottom and flowers at the top spilling out by the handle. I would hang them on the door, knock and run away! She was teaching me a Kingdom Principle: Love your Neighbor as Yourself Let us remember to model our marriages as well. A marriage in healing will heal a child as well. Craig Hill in *The Power of a Parent's Blessing* reminds us we were created to be God's Agents of Blessing to our children. A parent's blessing will change the life destiny of a child. These lessons are not only life-long for children. They restore harmony between the parents. When you openly forgive, you become a voice for God to those around you. Children will know this with their innate sense of what they observe which becomes more powerful than words themselves. If you have children and grandchildren, you will be well served to purchase this book. It will reveal the *seven critical times when a child needs to be blessed.*

JOURNAL NOW WHILE THIS IS FRESH ON YOUR MIND. REVIEW WITH REFLECTION TO HEAL THE WOUNDS

Are you holding anything against your partner with unforgiveness? Do you have the courage to identify it?

- Christ completely forgives us. Are you able to completely forgive your partner?

- Is your partner holding on to issues with unforgiveness? Are you holding on to an unforgiveness issue?

- Do you need to forgive yourself? This will release needed harmony from the Lord. Forgiveness blesses you.

- Do you regard yourself as an Ambassador of Harmony, offering forgiveness where it is needed?

- Ask the Holy Spirit to help you recall areas in your life where you need to repent and seek forgiveness.

- Recall a time when you forgave your partner of something. Did it bring you a sense of courage? Freedom? Release? Joy?

DECLARATION: Discipline me Lord to try and try again. Favor me with your opportunities to see where forgiveness is needed.

REFLECT ON THE FOLLOWING AND WRITE YOUR THOUGHTS IN YOUR PRAYER JOURNAL:

- YOUR WORDS TO JESUS

- IDEAS AND WORDS FROM JESUS

PRAYER: *Father God, I stand on the promise of your word found in* **Psalm 23** *that you "restore my soul" and "lead me in the paths of righteousness." Lord, I repent of any actions I may have taken that opened the doors in my life to the enemy, especially regarding my partner. I thank you for the sacrifice of Your Son, Jesus Christ. I thank you, Father, that heaven is divinely orchestrating situations and circumstances for the salvation of my family and loved ones. In Yeshua's Precious Name, I speak that every broken family relationship will be repaired by the love of God. I ask that a spirit of forgiveness and meekness be poured out upon my immediate and extended family through me. In Jesus Mighty and Precious Name, Amen.*

Chapter 6
CONFIDENCE

Lead Us From Temptation

SIFT AND SHIFT YOUR UNION WITH CONFIDENCE— DO NOT FOLLOW THE CROWD

CHEF NOTE: Sometimes, I think moms and cooks beg for temptations to just go out for dinner every now and then. The daily cooking of meals constantly begs for what's next. I find myself already thinking about tomorrow's menus the day before. I recall feeling tempted one year to throw in the towel for a Thanksgiving Dinner when we first started living aboard our boat, Escapade. (This calls for another novella—Kansas Girl gets Sea Legs.) Yes, back to dining aboard! The oven, only slightly bigger than a bread box, functioned as storage. How in the world would I cook a turkey! A new Bon Appetit magazine arrived with the answer…a stuffed turkey roll. Then I changed my mind and went with my delicious Wildrice Chicken Casserole. Easy to prepare and loved by all. I put aside the impressive turkey roll for a family favorite. It allowed more time to relax and enjoy the day at home, not a restaurant. We just prefer a family meal at home for one of the most precious of American Holidays. Such a day of thanksgiving for so much the Lord has given us. Thank goodness I gave up on booking our lovely meal with some other cook! Sometimes temptation comes from not doing something and certainly from opting for it. It has to do with the confidence to stick with something and not give up.

My example pales compared to the more significant issues of life. However, never give up applies to everything Christ desires for us because Christ never gives up on us. It calls for self-discipline. Why? He is never giving up on us! It begs you to set aside that which no longer serves you to make room for Him. Never give in to the temptation to quit. It might be that you need to leave something *like following the crowd*. Or maybe what boundary needs to be set. It is sticking with our beloved partners with trust in the Lord as our compass and guide to navigate life. Let Yeshua become the anchor of your soul. Don't make a move without His Holy Spirit! PS...I include this holiday/any day recipe in the back. This is awesome, a family favorite, and for sure will become yours as well.

Only God is my Source and my Provider who wastes nothing. Daily, I thank the Lord for leading me away from temptations. Remember what causes you to step into temptation means stepping in an idol. It is His *unfailing love* at work in your heart that will keep you without the desire to turn away. Remember it is *through the heart* we know God. No one loves us more than Yeshua. To *follow* Yeshua/Jesus means to *Love God* and *Love God's People*. Derek Prince in his "Orphans, Widows, the Poor and Oppressed," reminds us of this very thing. To love is to bless others. He reminds us as well the key to happiness is *not being loved*, it is having *someone to love*. Oh, my goodness. Did this ever speak to my heart about my beloved. He suggests loving someone is exciting and there are people not very far from you who need your love!!! Hello! Your beloved partner! Each of us must undergo God's refining process to grow spiritually. He clearly paid for you and me with His Body and Blood on the cross. He became our sin. Temptations can lead us to step away from Him. His Love will bring us back. We all have attractions that can bring a slow death. A slow death stops progress. It could be a slow death of trust. Or integrity. Or even a marriage. This is where the Holy Spirit's conviction steps in, keeping us on a Godly Path. Now, looking back, I can see my own slow death as it happened. I found myself leaning on my own understanding, which created a hardship. (**Proverbs 3:5-6**) God has a fantastic way of turning it around and making trials into something for good. (**Romans 8:28**) God turned the error of misplaced trust by delivering me through a difficult time in our marriage. As I shared earlier, I thank God for exposing me to the truth. Knowing God directs our steps released a new chapter in my life and that of my partner. (**Psalm 143:7**) He healed the shame in my heart and bound up my wounds with His Love.

God's Loving Guidance comes in so many ways, such as Holy Spirit Intuition. Looking back, I see my ego was tempted by the enemy away from God as my source. I needed to go through a death experience to renew my faith and trust in God. The reality was revealed. Yes, the Lord finally delivered me from this temptation. (**Psalm 107:21-22**) Through increased *trust and confidence*, God began to place me on a new path. (**Psalm 32: 7-8**) Once I released the past, a new door opened. My trust in God became more vital than ever, especially in this new time and season Confidence backed by courage was in place to trust the Lord and Holy Spirit to reveal my next steps. I persevered to endure the regrets about my marriage to transform them into my joy. This book became my healing Balm of Gilead. The entire endeavor from conception to printing became a time of healing on so many levels. God will always use you right where you are planted. Nothing wasted.

"I will instruct you and teach you in the way you should go; I will counsel you with my loving eye on you."

—Psalm 32:8 (NIV)

"Let us not become weary in doing good, for at the proper time we will reap a harvest if we do not give up."

—Galatians 6:9 (NIV)

"So now we draw near freely and boldly to where grace is enthroned, to receive mercy's kiss and discover the grace we urgently need to strengthen us in our time of weakness."

—Hebrews 4:16 (TPT)

"Therefore, as God's chosen people, holy and dearly loved, clothe yourselves with compassion, kindness, humility, gentleness and patience. Bear with each other and forgive one another if any of you has a grievance against someone. Forgive as the Lord forgave you. And over all these virtues put on love, which binds them all together in perfect unity."

—Colossians 3:12-14 (NIV)

TIME WASTED OR REDEEMED

In the early years of our marriage, my husband traveled a great deal. So, my time wrapped around my daughter, my projects, and our home during the week. *My precious daughter is from my first marriage.* The weekends brought us much treasured together time. Now, 40 years later, we are together all the time. It became shockingly apparent how vastly different we each spend our personal time. Can you guess?

He thinks of mine as being wasted. I, on the other hand, fully believe my time to be redeemed with eternal value. So, when together, time took on a whole new meaning. Oh yes! Maybe you know just what I mean. Suddenly having him home all the time shifted everything. In the early days of his retirement, I set the rule of leisurely breakfast, my dear husband must provide lunch, and I, your lovely wife, will take care of dinner. You can buy your assigned meal or make it. So slowly, the time boundaries were being set. Soon, all fell into place with his and my moving through a new and highly valued life together. He did what he wanted with his time, and I did mine. The years have passed, the activities slowly reduced, so again, *time* differences appeared. I desired to devote time to my spiritual growth and the Lord's Calling. Early rising was the answer. I bring this up because I needed to preserve my time to adjust to making more significant time with him. I desired to make every day count with time together to laugh, share and care for each other. I wanted our good days to be a blessing. Honestly, during these glorious days and times I always had his salvation on the back of my mind. My shift was to be more structured with him throughout the day. My early rising allowed me to continue to work on what I have been called to do and create quality time with him as well. Yes, in case you are wondering, I do all the cooking. I wouldn't have it any other way. Yes, our routine today is quieter, and you know what? All good all the time with the Lord. My partner was becoming receptive to my changes through silently being blessed by me. Setting a boundary allows each of us to follow our joy with the Lord. (**Acts 17:26-27**) We decided to set new boundaries around other things, such as letting go of an abundance of possessions. We decided it was time to simplify.

"You will seek me and find me when you seek me with all your heart. I will be found by you," declares the Lord, "and will bring you back from captivity."

—Jeremiah 29:13-14 (NIV)

DOWNSIZE AND SIMPLIFY

A change came with downsizing. Worldly goods and possession are an idol for many people, cars, clothes, and who knows. With a shift in career and business-building years, we decided to downsize and simplify. I just didn't realize how much I had gathered and collected over the years serving our active lifestyle. Now, we no longer entertained corporately. It all seemed so burdensome. (**Matthew 6:19**) I called a caterer friend and gave everything to her for her business. I could not believe the amount of stuff I let go. What seemed so precious (idolized) went to storage. Guess what? Four years later, not to mention dollars lost, we let go of all of it because it just didn't matter any longer. So, the remainder became a burden as well. Condo living, which we said we would never do, became the solution to simplify. When the day the Lord comes, these possessions will have little meaning. My friends, focus on building your treasure up in heaven, not earth. Take time one day to look around you. What can you release to increase your new spiritual understanding? Let the Hand of God move over your heart.

Once again, on the move. Mentioned earlier, the day finally came to sell our unit and relocate up two floors to where we now live. A force took over me as I moved all the kitchen, clothes, and art pieces with a cart and clothing rack. The heavy things were being transferred the next day. All was going smoothly until and unfortunately, the marble from the living room coffee table slipped off the cart right at the elevator. Now in a thousand pieces, I took a deep breath and asked if the floor was damaged. No, it was fine. Thank you, Jesus. With great disappointment on the guy's faces, I quickly shifted my viewing it all as, hey, it is just a piece of marble. No one had lost their life here. We cleaned up the mess together. I keep one part of my formerly treasured marble top in my pantry area, which I see daily. It reminds me to let go of idols. (**1 John 5:21**) I tipped the movers at the end of the day despite this event. A blessing comes with all our experiences. This was not their mistake so much as a test for me to see how I would respond. Brian, the owner, offered to replace and asked to meet at a particular time to see what could be done. The next day I called him to let him know I changed my mind. I didn't need to have it replaced. Relief was audible over the phone. To me, this was a sign of spiritual maturity.

Our storage unit became the next great cleansing. We let go of those *someday I will need* non-essentials. I arranged for Faith Farms Ministry to come and take it away. It is such a temptation to hang on to stuff thinking you may need this. I recall a great rule regarding my closet. If not worn at all in a year, someone else will wear it so give it away. My daughter came for the weekend after our initial move to the condo and brought her Marie Kondo's books, *The Life-Changing Magic of Tidying Up* and *Spark Joy*. Marie's delightful books offer the true solution about releasing items. Keep it only if it brings you joy. Every item in the home must be regarded this way. This means clothes, books, papers, kitchen items, pictures, and pillows. We spent the whole weekend loving the process of discovering joy. Then, to those items being kept, Marie offers a special way to organize them. You just can't imagine the joy this brought to me not to mention the bonding moments of being with my daughter. To this day, I look at the organized drawers with such feelings of joy. It brings me astonishing joy I tell you. It brought a sense of order to It is very important to have agreements about letting go with our partners because release will shift the atmosphere creating new levels of trust! (**Isaiah 43:18-19**) Letting go clears the way for a new thing.

Letting go reveals so much about your partner or yourself. It was easy for me to release and for my partner, not easy at all. To this day, he hangs on to things. That is his great temptation. Letting go of all the storage items wasn't so easy for him. He wanted to keep his skis and poles! Letting go applies to so many things of life. Forgiveness comes to mind here. I bring this up to caution you on this area of letting go of the past because it can be such a difficult road to travel. This is where the Lord steps in to direct your next moves for Him. It will always call for a new wineskin. (**Matthew 9:17**) With *confidence*, this significant reduction of possessions helped us both find a new sense of freedom. No more anger over what to keep and what and what to release We sold our home and moved to a condo and found our more simplified life to enjoy. Giving up the former treasures gave us a newly found contentment. (**Isaiah 43:18-19**) Move forward in confidence to know what you have become, not what you don't have. Release what holds you back.

"Be alert and guard your heart from greed and from always wishing for what you don't have. For your life can never be measured by the amount of things you possess."

—Luke 12:15 (TPT)

"Forget the former things; do not dwell on the past."

—Isaiah 43:18 (NIV)

CLEANSE THE HOME OF THE OCCULT

When you awaken, you will need to look around your home. You will recall my slow entrance into yet sustained living with New Age thinking. I thank God for the day a dear friend shared an article from Derek Prince on the importance of cleansing the home of any occult possessions. Why I seemed to have something of everything on that list. Buddhas come to mind as well as books. I had a statue which I loved that suddenly I found glaring at me. Gone. My husband never knew that day of my great purging. (**Deuteronomy 18:10-11**) Yet I tell you, *I felt* the difference immediately. Much of the angst and anger over things quieted down. A sense of peace descended over me. I created my own problem by collecting these things. I opened that door to the occult. Not him. Honestly, I had no idea the powerful vibrations these items carry from those who created them. I cannot stress enough to look over your home. A painting I had done of a black Madonna went into the trash. I even got rid of some knitted cats, just to be sure. I was relentless in my search for things. Books, jewelry, pottery pieces, to name a few. (**2 Corinthians 7:1**) It all seemed so right when I was tempted. Many prophets now urge us to cleanse our home in the natural and close all the demonic entrances, in Jesus' Name. (**1 John 4:3**) New levels of your personal confidence will urge you to make new choices with Holy Spirit discernment.

"Trust in the Lord with all your heart and lean not on your own understanding;
In all your way submit to him and he will make your paths straight."

—Proverbs 3:5-6 (NIV)

No one should say "God is tempting me—" goes on to say. "…for God is incapable of being tempted by evil and he is never the source of temptation. Instead, it is each person's own desires and thoughts that drag them into evil and lure them away into darkness. Evil desires give birth to evil actions. And when sin is fully mature it can murder you! So, my friends, don't be fooled by your own desires!"

—James 1:13-16 (TPT)

"You can rationalize it all you want and justify the path of error you have chosen, but you'll find out in the end that you took the road to destruction."

—Proverbs 14:12 (TPT)

THE SLIPPERY SLOPE OF CHOICES

Marriage partners will need to make choices. Lots of them. How you make them matters with or without the Lord. Some become a slippery slope of choices that will later compromise a marriage. I read somewhere on average, we make 35,000 choices a day, and God Himself knows about every one of them. Your preferences made with a Kingdom Mindset causes the Lord to rejoice. This pleases Him. Exceedingly, He Rejoices with those made in humility. He greatly opposes the one focused on self-pride. A relocation decision comes to mind that forever changed our lives. After 30+ years of living in our home back East, we felt it was time to leave, which upset our family. One summer, we put our house on the market. It took two years for the sale to become a reality. Looking back, I realize the Lord's timing is what prevailed. (**Proverbs 19:21**) Leaning on our own understanding proved a mistake that forever can take us on a path of problems. It was like a domino effect. Suffice to say, hindsight always allows this perspective so necessary for spiritual refinement. Commit to the Lord whatever you do, and he will establish your plans. The recovery began with repentance. Make sure on all large and significant decisions to have not only scripture to guide you and at least one or better two witnesses to make sure this is the Lord's Will for you. Let the Lord help you.

Make sure you exalt the Lord to give Him all glory in helping you make good choices. As mentioned, seek several witnesses especially for big decisions. Awaken to the guiding thoughts of the Holy Spirit, leading you to bear fruitful outcomes. Repent quickly for the unwanted consequences. The Lord gives us free will and choices to create life, not death. With Jesus, we move with discernment into life-giving decisions. His love sustains me to make them righteously with confidence which brings peace and contentment. Remember to place on the altar of your heart your choices so they will contribute to the Kingdom. (**Matthew 6:31**) Our choices will become miracles from the Lord. Walking together in this way, our partners begin to see how the Lord's Favor brings a miracle blessing.

"Trust in the Lord completely, and do not rely on our own opinions. With all your heart rely on him to guide you, and he will lead you in every decision you make. Become intimate with him in whatever you do and he will lead you wherever you go."

—Proverbs 3:5-6 (TPT)

"God opposes the proud but shows favor to the humble."

—James 4:6 (NIV)

"We all experience times of testing which is normal for every human being. But God will be faithful to you. He will screen and filter the severity, nature ad timing of every test or trial you face so that you can bear it. And each test is an opportunity to trust him more, for along with every trial God has provided for you, a way of escape that will bring you out of it victoriously."

—1 Corinthians 10:13 (TPT)

"Praise be to the God and Father of our Lord Jesus Christ! In his great mercy he has given us new birth into a living hope through the resurrection of Jesus Christ from the dead."

—1 Peter 1:3 (NIV)

EXPECT A MIRACLE AND BE A MIRACLE BY WALKING IN THE SPIRIT.

Holy Spirit's guiding voice will alert you in your choices. I expect the joy of a miracle every day in my life and my marriage. I bless and pray my beloved to be saved. I wish the Lord to bring love and restoration to my husband's heart. Remember, the heart is what the Lord examines. I expect my darling to wake up every morning a new person. I seek Holy Spirit to give me new insights to fulfill His Purpose for him. I greet the day in Love and desire to succeed with Love. I usher in a holy boldness to become a Lioness out in the world, making a difference. I pray and intercede where led. I ask for exceptional help to lay down myself and walk in humility with the Holy Spirit. I must look at my pride and laugh at how ridiculous it is. Who do I think I am kidding? Show me, Lord, how to use my voice to bear fruit for you. Don't let me miss an opportunity to be your servant for another. (**Galatians 5:13**) Help me, Lord, to love the thing you love and walk away from the things you hate, like gossip. (**Proverbs 6:16-19**) May Holy Spirit show me my errors for me to repent and corrected to be forgiven. Help me soar, Lord like the Eagle, to be renewed daily by you. Open my eyes, Lord, to see the cracks in my foundation where the enemy could come in. Give me compassion, Lord, for others to see Christ in me. Let me be a miracle for them to make You, their fortress. Let me help them see the wonder of your Glory, especially my beloved. When I have reset my mind with these words, temptations, especially with my marriage, diminish. Miracles come when you least expect them.

"For I know the plans I have for you," declares the Lord, "Plans to prosper you and not to harm you, plans to give you hope and a future."

—Jeremiah 29:11 (NIV)

"If your faith remains strong, even while surrounded by life's difficulties, you will continue to experience the untold blessings of God! True happiness comes as you pass the test with faith and receive the victorious crown of life promised to every lover of God!"

—James 1:12 (TPT)

YOUR JOURNAL MUST BE AMAZING BY NOW.
Continue to REVIEW with REFLECTION:

- Is there an area of your life that has become an idol? With humility, can you be honest about this?

- Have you been trivial in pursuing that which looks like gold?

- What is the price you have paid to pursue trivial things? What about them still holds your attention?

- Have your possessions become a burden?

- Do you turn to Holy Spirit to lead you on your path to begin to say no to things of the world?

- Consider how choosing to trust the Lord's plan and purpose for your life will empower your relationship with your partner?

- Do you rejoice over everything and pray continuously?

DECLARTION: *I decree today Holy Spirit reveals those things that waste my time, talents, and precious gifts. Thank you, Lord for showing me this.*

REFLECT ON THE FOLLOWING AND WRITE YOUR THOUGHTS IN YOUR PRAYER JOURNAL:

- YOUR WORDS TO JESUS

- IDEAS AND WORDS FROM JESUS

PRAYER: *Precious Lord Jesus, come to me with awareness of where I have chosen to compromise over the steadfastness of your love. Help me, Lord, to lead me from temptations to restore my soul with your Presence. Lead me in the right paths, Lord, for your Righteousness Name Sake. You are my Shepherd, Lord. Thank you, Jesus, for covering my family with your precious Blood of the Lamb for cleansing and protection from the temptations of a fallen world. Oh Lord, forgive me for any wrongdoing that caused me to step away from you. Lord, I am so very grateful. In Your Matchless and Precious name Lord, Amen.*

Chapter 7
CONVICTION

Deliver Us From Evil

SIFT AND SHIFT YOUR UNION WITH CONVICTION. REAL LIFE HAS TROUBLES

CHEF NOTE: One fall, we were headed South on Escapade coming through New York City, and of course, the Statue of Liberty was right there. Such a lovely day for travel, quickly making it through NYC and back out to the ocean about 1 o'clock in the afternoon. So, the usual place to stop for the night came up quickly, and we said, what the heck? Let us keep going. Atlantic City, New Jersey, was our destination. By 4:00 p.m., we knew we had made a mistake. Trouble ahead for sure. We did not listen to our intuition for the Lord's advice on the weather. How could we know what was ahead?

The Lord knew, however. A wrong decision. Skies darkened, and the sea was building up with challenging traveling conditions. We arrived at the inlet well after 10PM, and there in the pitch dark began more trouble. Terrible waves crashing against us, heaving us up and down from side to side. The troughs were so deep I could see the ocean nearly covering our windows. Captain hubby had gone to the top deck to steer better while he had me brace myself in the tiny bathroom off the galley.

I heard the refrigerator shift and open along with cabinets emptying and crashing food to the floor. Nothing remained stationary. Finally, the movement stopped abruptly as we slowly, with caution, made it through the inlet to the inner harbor. Thank you, Lord, for your inner harbor of safety. Prayers to heaven for hubby to be okay and still with me. He came down the stairway from the upper deck with joyous relief and deep gratitude to the Father. We wept. Jesus wept. (**John 11:35**) We could not stop crying for joy that we made it. We were safe! Thank you, Heavenly Father, the Anchor of our Soul. Oh, the mess.

Sometimes cooks have troubles, you know! Like galley disasters! Yet, such a time for *thanksgiving.* The mess we could clean up. The food we could replace. The Kitchen with the kitchener always survives through faith and prayer. Keeping prayer, a priority will aid you in your life. *Help me Jesus* is a good one. *Thank you, Jesus,* another! God turns all things, including troubles, into good. My belief served me well. I just knew we would be okay. God was with us. My beloved husband was safe.

"What then, shall we say in response to these things? If God is for us, who can be against us?"

—Romans 8:36 (NIV)

"I will never leave you nor forsake you."

—Joshua 1:5 (NIV)

"And when they climbed into the boat, the wind died down"

—Matthew 14:32 (NIV)

WALK IN PRAISE AND THANKSGIVING

The greater your trust in the Lord's compassion for you, the more quickly you will remain unshaken by troubles. His compassion becomes your default response. We can agree misfortunes come. The danger comes from many places. Praise of the Lord and worship to the Lord help me contend with contentment to remain unshaken when trouble comes. My prophetic author friend, Leah Dent, shared a word from the Lord on problems. On a recent walking trip, she asked the Lord how to climb the hills of the day. Approach all things first with praise. She shared write praise on one foot and thanksgiving on the other. You approach a mountain of trouble one step at a time with praise and thanksgiving. She was given (**Psalm 68:1**) for the Lord to scatter her enemies and deepen her understanding. Write on your feet today. Praise on the Left and Thanksgiving on the right as you walk through any mountain of trouble. (**Psalm 118:6**) God goes with you. Be not afraid.

Let no troubling news shake you. The Holy Spirit helps me to be unshaken in my marriage regardless of the situation. (**Isaiah 54:10**) Here, the gift of forbearance graces you with intuition to sort out the trouble. Fixing your eyes on the Lord helps you build *conviction* into a solid faith to *stay in the moment*. (**Hebrews 12:2**) Staying in the moment keeps you from going to the past and a list of accounts or moving ahead to tomorrow's worries. Yes, when I put the Lord Jesus first in all things, keeping my eyes and ears on the prize becomes my default position. Finally, prayers to the heavens, for nothing is impossible with the Lord. His *unfailing love* sets my path straight. (**Luke 1:37**) Let us understand the enemy detests the Lord's most intimidating weapon: "Worship!" Active worship creates the Joy of the Lord, who becomes your strength and the enemy's weakness. Praise and worship become a vehicle to generate confidence in your convictions. (**Psalm 150:1-2**) Prayer is the glue that puts it all into place, helping us to see and hear clearly.

"All praises belong to the God and Father of our Lord Jesus Christ. For he is the Father of tender mercy and God of endless comfort. He always comes alongside us to comfort us in every suffering so that we can come alongside those who are in any painful trial. We can bring them this same comfort that God has poured out upon us."

—2 Corinthians 1:3-4 (TPT)

"And everything I've taught you is so that the peace which is in me will be in you and will give you great confidence as you rest in me. For in this unbelieving world you will experience trouble and sorrows, but you must be courageous for I have conquered the world!"

—John 16:33 (TPT)

"God! Arise with awesome power and every one of your enemies will scatter in fear!"

—Psalm 68:1 (TPT)

"Not one promise from God is empty of power. Nothing is impossible with God!"

—Luke 1:37 (TPT)

"Refuse to worry about tomorrow, but deal with each challenge that comes your way one day at a time. Tomorrow will take care of itself."

—Matthew 6:34 (TPT)

"Though the mountains be shaken and the hills be removed, yet my unfailing love for you will not be shaken nor my covenant of peace be removed," says the Lord, who has compassion on you.

—Isaiah 54:10 (NIV)

"I will instruct you and teach you in the way you should go; I will counsel you with my loving eye on you."

—Psalm 32:8 (NIV)

"Love is patient, love is kind. It does not envy, it does not boast, it is not proud. It does not dishonor others, it is not self-seeking. It is not easily angered it keeps no record of wrongs. Love does not delight in evil but rejoices with the truth. It always protects, always trusts, always hopes, always perseveres."

—1 Corinthians 13:4-7 (NIV)

"Peace I leave give to you; my peace if give you. I do not give to you as the world gives. Do not let your hearts be troubled and do not be afraid."

—John 14:27 (TPT)

GUARDING MY EYE GATES AND EAR GATES

The body's members clearly can add to the trouble or be a solution for it. In **Romans 6:13** Paul gives us teachings and warnings about our eyes and ears. What does this say to us who are on the path to do the right things? It begs us to watch what we allow our eyes to see and our ears to hear. Seek only to want what the Lord wants to do through these body members. Use discernment to draw the line and make boundaries. I recently drew the line with the TV news. I simply refused to watch any of it to prevent my gates from becoming fearful which is what the enemy wants! Walk away from all the things the Lord hates (**Proverbs 6:16-19**). For example, make a rule for yourself about gossip. Remember, if someone draws you in to stir up trouble, they will also bring you trouble. The enemy will use your gates to support his lies and masterful ability to divide a house. Let the Lord be the judge of such deceitfulness. (**Psalm 7:11**) The enemy will also use our partners or those around us to do the same thing. Ultimately and importantly, only put in front of you *"what you want to become."* Remember you are an ambassador for the Lord who brings to the Kingdom encouragement not discouragement. This takes conviction. Feed your soul with the Living Word to be revived! Declare boldly to speak to the dark forces. Take an example of the enemy wants to steal my hope. Say: *I break off the lie of having no hope and rebuke it now in the Powerful Name of Jesus.* (**Psalm 25:4-5**) Teach me your ways, Lord. Soon you will be known by what you seek and speak. The boundaries you set become who you are. Your name becomes associated with how you walk this out. We can all see the world has lost its way. Be the one who knows all things are possible with Jesus.

It all looks impossible. During these days of darkness in the world, I remain in trust that the plans of the Lord will be revealed in wondrous ways. Through repentance, restoration, and restitution He heals the land and brings *Unity* among His people. (**Isaiah 61:7**) Watching everything we say and do will contribute to restoration or block it. The Lord never wastes anything and will turn this into His Good for His Glory. You are called by the Lord to fix your eyes on Him. We can move in revelation through the eyes and ears for how we become the "Daily Bread" for another. Daily, present to the Lord, your members to be under His Dominion over all our senses: see, hear, say, know, feel, and smell with your eyes, ears, mouth, hands, heart, feet, body, spirit, and soul. As you begin to clear the Body Temple honoring the Lord God of your being, you deepen your discernments in all things. (**1 Corinthians 6:19-20**) Together, these create your personal vision of the Lord, which sustains you, preventing troubling distractions such as the news. The *cleansed soul* then advances into a mighty destiny and plan of the Lord. You have something *only you* can speak that will heal others. He has plans to prosper you and help you see your life has a purpose. (**Jeremiah 29:11**) Stepping into your destiny all begins with your gates. This places in you a higher frequency untouched by a lower frequency of the world. Step into your future by stepping out of those things your eyes and ears should not see nor hear. Your choices will affect your partner and lift him up to a higher perspective because you have done the same thing for yourself. It takes you out of what once you considered normal to a new spiritual dimension. The Lord's patterns will always begin first in the natural and then proceed to the spiritual. Only the Lord's Spirit can bring us to victory.

"So then, refuse to answer its call to surrender your body as a tool for wickedness. Instead, passionately answer God's call to keep yielding your body to him as one who has now experienced resurrection life! You live now for his pleasure ready to be used by his noble purpose."

—Romans 6:13 (TPT)

"And we know that in all things God works for the good of those who love him, who have been called according to his purpose."

—Romans 8:28 (NIV)

"There are six evils God truly hates and a seventh that is an abomination to him. Putting others down while considering yourself superior, spreading lies and rumors, spilling the blood of the innocent, plotting evil in our heart towards another, gloating over doing what's plainly wrong, sprouting lies in false testimony and stirring up strife between friends. These are entirely despicable to God!"

—Proverbs 6:16-19 (TPT)

"Do not offer any part of yourself to sin as an instrument of wickedness but rather offer yourself to God as those who have been brought from death to life; and offer every part of yourself to him as an instrument of righteousness. For sin shall no longer be your master because you are not under the law but under grace."

—Romans 6:13-14 (NIV)

TURN OFF THE NEWS TO TUNE INTO A HIGHER FREQUENCY

Turn off the news to tune into the Lord's frequency. Fake news dominates the airwaves. What you believe requires discernment to filter out the truth in today's announcements. The spirit of deception works overtime in our world. Higher frequencies reveal the gifts from a higher understanding for needed wisdom to remain alert in our marriage. The lower the frequency, the greater the heaviness of it. During the years, we have had several troubling times with family dynamics. Sorting them out calls for a reset of your thinking from a higher perspective. Instead of blame and shame, move into addressing the enemy's lies to steal and destroy your family relationships. Be bold to say yes to unity with your partner and family with a no to the world's chaos. Satan loves addictions and misuse of the body temple. Quietly and daily break off the yoke of Satan off your partner. (**1 Peter 5:8**) I have used intercessory prayer with my prayer groups to assist me. When we are walking with an unbeliever, support becomes essential to hear the truth. Coming away with the Lord stimulates the best way to hear from Him. (**Mark 6:31**) Even a ten-minute pause with coffee will remarkably refresh you. Your silence allows Him to caress you with His Love. Today we have so many ways to feel the Presence of the Lord. Soaking Music, for sure, lifts your frequency. It takes you to another level even while you might be doing other things such as cooking. Keep it on low as a background. I play meditation music every morning. It plays all day, and finally, at bedtime I turn it off. I use this as a background while doing tasks. Such a good and soothing sound. Or how about listening to the bible while you are driving. Maybe even during your sleep. Your senses can be affected, especially with *feeling* His Presence. I maintain it is *a feeling* that reveals His guidance. Go higher to feel and focus more. Remember, you are addressing yourself first. You are vital to shifting your family through being a spiritual example. As your walk with the Holy Spirit deepens, you will have clarity when He surrounds you.

"The mind governed by the flesh is death, but the mind governed by the spirit is life and peace."

—**Romans 8:6** (NIV)

FOCUS AND CLARITY PREVENT DISTRACTIONS.

Don't let you mind wander. It creates an opening for the thief to come in and take charge. If I allow negative thinking, for sure, I will find trouble at my door. It opens the door for responding negatively to remarks from my partner. How I handle them will manifest with the words I use. Holy Spirit Power fills my mouth with words. (**Acts 1:8**)

Help me to remain silent to allow time for me to pray. Help me, Holy Spirit, to receive your spiritual weapons for taking those strongholds within my partner to captivity. Realize the enemy often makes an unbeliever captive by him. Christ was sent to proclaim the release of the prisoners from these prisons. (**Luke 4:18**) The Lord wants to announce this release through your mouth! (**2 Corinthians 10:3-5**) This passage provides an effective prayer to have the Divine Power demolish strongholds. *Verse 5 Demolishing every pretension that sets itself up against the knowledge of God and to take captive every thought to make it obedient to Christ.* You punish every act of disobedience displayed by your obedience to pray. Rebuke in the Name of Jesus! I use this passage any time the enemy tries to break into my Fortress of the Lord. Not long again I had a odd exchange with someone that just wouldn't leave me. I asked the Holy Spirit how to handle this situation. The answer came: Bless her. My blessing became a prayer releasing any anxious thoughts and by prayer with thanksgiving to present it to the Christ Mind. (**Philippians 4:4-7**) Cast to the Christ Mind what you cannot handle then begin blessing that person. Forgiving that person. You plant the seed and let Jesus grow the tree. (**Romans 4:17**) This passage reminds us of Abraham's faith in the God Promises. Even though it looks hopeless, God calls into being things that don't exist yet!!! Calls them as though they were. The very situation causing me strife turning into a blessing bringing peace to me. This prayer will help you endure these trials with your marriage. One day, the Holy Spirit will turn them into great joy, not a new test of wills. Expect and be convinced whatever you are suffering *will change.* (**Psalm 27:13**) Remain confident that you will see the *goodness of the Lord* Press forward in prayer no matter what!

"Consider it pure joy, my brothers and sisters, whenever you face trials of many kinds. Because you know that the testing of your faith produces perseverance. Let perseverance finish its work so that you may be mature and complete, not lacking anything."

—James 1:2 (NIV)

"Don't worry or surrender to your fear. For you've believed in God, now trust and believe in me also."

—John 14:1 (TPT)

God is Love. There is no fear in love. We cannot express this enough. Whoever lives in His Love lives in God and God in them. (**1 John 4:18**) When troubles appear, place a 911 call for supernatural help from the Lord! I cast to the Christ Mind all my concerns for Him to do my battles. (**Exodus 14:14**) Stay calm. Turning concerns over to His Mind will immediately bring relief. He reads my tears like a book. Once a problematic exchange starts or tears come, I silently call to Jesus for help. I know, and so do you, the Wisdom of God far outweighs our own. His ways are higher than ours. (**Isaiah 58:8-9**) Ask in His Name, and He will answer. (**John 14:13-14**) God can do more than we could imagine. God's love helps us deal with difficult moments of fear or concern. When there is the reluctance to address a situation, then for sure, it grows into a "Mountain of Troubles." (**Zechariah 4:6-7**) Remember, with God, all obstacles are possible. (**Luke 1:37**) Remember my friend Leah Dent's advice on Praise. God told her to write Praise on the left foot and Thanksgiving on the right. Take one step at a time to clear the way. Prayer and praise with thanksgiving restores my trust, preventing distractions from shifting me. Time alone to Wait on the Lord begins the healing. (**Psalm 27:14**) Steal away to love the Lord for reflection and restoration. Make yourself stop to take time with Him.

His Perfect Love casts out all fear. Love brings faith to our trust in God for all things. Walk by faith not by sight to please the Lord in all you do.

"If you keep my commands, you will remain in my love, just as I have kept my Father's commands and remain in his love."

—John 15:10 (NIV)

"Those who sow their tears as seeds will reap a harvest with joyful shouts of glee. They may weep as they go out carrying their seed to sow but they will return with joyful laugher and shouting with gladness as they bring back armloads of blessing and a harvest overflowing."

—Psalm 126:5-6 (TPT)

"You are rising like the perfectly fitted stones of the temple and your lives have been built up together upon the foundations laid by my apostles and prophets, and best of all, you are connected to the head Cornerstone of the building the Anointed One, Jesus Christ himself."

—Ephesians 3:20 (TPT)

"So Lord don't hold back your love or withhold your tender mercies from me. Keep me in your truth and let your compassion overflow to me no matter what I face."

—Psalm 40:11 (TPT)

"But realize this: if a homeowner had known what time of night the burglar would come to his house, he would have been alert and ready and not let his house be robbed. So always be ready, alert and prepared because at an hour when you're not expecting him, the Son of Man will come."

—Matthew 24:43 (TPT)

DAILY PRAYERS AND COMMUNION OFFERS INTIMACY AND PROTECTION

Young families today must guard against their children being exposed to mind-grabbing forces. Train a young child the way he should go, and he will not depart from it. (**Proverbs 22:6**) Teach them to read the Word along with daily prayer. Set an example for them. Daily prayer provides the necessary protection (**Psalm 91**) to crush the strongholds of the dark side for our partners as well. (**2 Corinthians 10:5**) Daily Communion delivers the elements of protection and cleansing. Everything about God is wrapped up in the Blood of Christ. (**Matthew 26:26-28**) We seek to be forgiven, healed, cleansed, and sanctified with His Body and His Blood through Communion. The shed Blood of Yeshua emits Power to atone for sins. It emits protection from the Blood of the Lamb against the enemy. Have *conviction saying no* to the enemy with Holy Spirit Power.

"Consider it pure joy, my brothers and sisters whenever you face trials of many kinds, because you know that the testing of your faith produces perseverance."

—James 1:2-3 (NIV)

Rejoice always to stay aligned with the Holy Spirit. Thank the Father for sending His Son for our Salvation. The shed blood of Yeshua equips us with everything good for doing His Will. (**Hebrews 13:20-21**). He became our sin. He sent us the Holy Spirit Power to bless us. Embrace and submit to the Holy Spirit, and He will never leave you. He will always help you and comfort you and anchor you to Him. Immerse yourself in Him. Make no move without Him. Daily Communion coupled with the Holy Spirit Power clears your way for your entire household. Soon you will have intimacy with Him. Before all else, you must first have intimacy between Jesus and yourself. You are asking Jesus to come have an encounter with you. He learns your patterns. (**Galatians 5:25**) Mine is receiving through dreams and visions. As mentioned before, He knows I will google dream meanings to record in my Sacred Time journaling. The meanings are just stunning as comfort and support. For example, January 28th, I dreamt the night before of playing the violin, indicating harmony and contentment. This profound meaning was so welcomed because on the 28th day, we moved 2 floors up in our condo. This dream interpretation was on point to let me know harmony and contentment would follow the stress of moving. Yes, He knows me and guides me on which way to go. In Him alone, I trust. I thank Him for any covering of *conviction* of my stepping off the path.

Cover yourself with the full Armor of God to be strong in the Lord with His Mighty Power. When the day of evil comes, we must take a stand against the Devil's schemes. We struggle not against flesh but against the powers of darkness. Be ready with the Belt of Truth at your waist, the Breastplate of Righteousness over your heart, your feet fitted with readiness to share the Good News Gospel of peace and the Helmet of Salvation to guard your thinking. Finally, the Shield of Faith to stop the flaming arrows of the evil one and the double-edged Sword of the Spirit which is the Word of God for a blessing or protection (**Ephesians 6:10-17**) We need the full protection of God over our hearts, minds, and souls. Thank you, Jesus, for the *Holy Spirit Conviction* to protect us. Holy Spirit Power, coupled with our faith, helps us stay strong in the spirit with Daily Communion, the **23rd Psalm**, and **Psalm 91** Prayers of Protection over my children, home, and marriage. The Fortress of the Most High God becomes our hiding place.

"Be cheerful with joyous celebrations in every season of life. Let your joy overflow! And let gentleness be seen by every relationship for our Lord is ever near."

—Philippians 4:4-5 (TPT)

"The Thief comes to steal and kill and destroy; I have come that they have life; and have it to the full. I am the good shepherd. The good shepherd lays down his life for the sheep."

—John 10:10-11 (NIV) Thank you Jesus for rescuing me.

"That evening the people brought to him many who were demonized And by Jesus only speaking a word of healing over them, they were totally set free from their torment, and everyone who was sick received their healing. In doing this, Jesus fulfilled the prophecy of Isaiah: He put upon himself our weaknesses, and he carried away our diseases and made us well."

—Matthew 8:16-17 (TPT)

"When tempted, no one should say God is tempting me. For God cannot be tempted by evil, nor does he tempt anyone; but each person is tempted when they are dragged away by their own evil desire and enticed. Then after desire has conceived it gives birth to sin; and sin when it is full-grown gives birth to death."

—James 1:13-15 (NIV)

GIVE TROUBLES TO THE LORD.

I lean on the wisdom of God the Father. Having a Prayer Group offers much-needed support, especially when troubles arise. Where two or more are gathered in prayer, the Lord hears. Decrees on earth become a reality in heaven. (**Matthew 18:18**) We all must bind the enemy strongholds and loose Angelic Hosts to guide us. Prayer activates the *supernatural solutions* of the Lord to be revealed. Prayer will show many hidden things to help me move forward in my marriage. (**2 Corinthians 10:5**) Walking with an intention for the Lord offers another layer of protection. Again, I say, cast your troubles to the Mind of Christ. (**Psalm 55:22**) Let Him take care of your battles. (**1 Samuel 17:47**) Trust relentlessly in the Lord to handle all things. You plant the seed and let the Lord grow the tree. You will become like an olive tree planted by the living waters to encourage others. **Remember the battle belongs to the lord.**

"Do not be afraid or discouraged because of this vast army for the battle is not yours but God's."

—**2 Chronicles 20:15** (NIV)

"Therefore do not worry about tomorrow, for tomorrow will worry about itself. Each day has enough trouble of its own."

—**Matthew 6:34** (NIV)

"Do not let your hearts be troubled, you believe n God; believe also in me."

—**John 14:1** (NIV)

"They will not live in fear or dread of what may come for their hearts are firm even secure in their faith."

—Psalm 112:7 (TPT)

"In the midst of a very server trial, their overflowing joy and heir extreme poverty welled up in rich generosity."

—2 Corinthians 8:2 (NIV)

"If you bow low in God's awesome presence, he will eventually exalt you as you leave the timing in his hands. Pour out all your worries and stress upon him and leave them there, for he always tenderly cares for you."

—1 Peter 5:6-7 (TPT)

"So we are convinced that every detail of our lives is continually woven together for good, for we are his lovers who have been called to fulfill his destined purpose."

—Romans 8:28 (TPT)

NIV states:

"...for everyone born of God overcomes the world. This is the victory that has overcome the world even our faith."

BECOME AN AMBASSADOR FOR THE LORD, AN ENCOURAGER.

I encourage you to become an ambassador for the Lord in your marriage. Become the CEO of your family: Chief Encouragement Officer! A walking testimony for Him. As a Christ Follower, you will bring His Hope to everyone around you because of the courage you reveal with your heart, mind, and soul. Your close friends will soon see how you can change the atmosphere. (**2 Corinthians 5:20**) Expect a miracle and expect to be a miracle for your beloved. You can be a miracle for your partner as the Lord steps in to heal your union. Jesus has overcome the darkness of the world. (**John 16:33**) Trust Jesus that with faith your beloved's heart will begin softening. Soon and in a little while, the Lord lets you know salvation *only comes* from Him. (**John 3:17**) Your job becomes loving and forgiving your partner. You and I are His Light. Daily, declare you are a Child of God. Choose to be all in for God. Be resolute with courage, confidence, and conviction in all your conversations, silently blessing him. Pause to allow the Holy Spirit to show you with when you should speak and what to say.

Remember to stop, pray, and declare to change the atmosphere wherever you go. Be an intentional ambassador and CEO for the Lord. You may be the only bible a person ever knows. (**2 Corinthians 3:2-3**) Craig Hill in his Daily Scripture word speaks about all being supplied if you represent a country as an ambassador. Say you are appointed to be Ambassador for the United States to France. Everything, including where to reside, food, cars, necessary support would be automatically given allowing you to focus on your mission. It is the same today with being the Lord's Ambassador. You go out with intention answering your call to manifest the Kingdom. All will be supplied. The Lord will bring you the needed connections. So, remember, if the Lord assigns you, He will also equip you. (**Matthew 7:7**) Everyone who asks receives.

"You yourselves are our letter, written on our hearts, known and read by everyone. You show that you are a letter from Christ, the result of our ministry, written not with ink but with the Spirit of the living God, not on tablets of stone but on tablets of human hearts."

—2 Corinthians 3:2 (NIV)

"For I know the plans I have for you," declares the Lord "plans to prosper you and not to harm you, plans to give you hope and a future."

—Jeremiah 29:11 (NIV)

"Ask and it will be given to you; seek and you will find' nock and the door will be opened to you. For everyone who asks receives; the one who seeks finds; and to the one who knocks the door will be opened."

—Matthew 7:7-8 (NIV)

"I will answer your cry for help every time you pray, and you will feel my presence in your time of trouble. I will deliver you and bring you honor."

—Psalm 91:15 (TPT)

"I have told you these things, so that in me your may have peace. In this world you will have trouble. But take heart! I have overcome the world."

—John 16:33 (NIV)

AWESOME MY FRIEND…YOU STAY WITH THIS!!!

Review and Rejoice!

- Can you identify recent trouble for its cause? Do they involve your partner and his choices?

- Are you able to cast troubles to the Christ Mind then trust enough with conviction to let it go?

- Are you ready to release a troubled area to let it become your testimony of and to the Lord?

- Will, you allow the refining fire of the Lord to purge you and prepare you as His Bride?

- Do you guard your mind and your thoughts against the enemy?

Write out your plan to identify the sources of troubles in your life. In your Marriage and in your family life. Then let the Holy Spirit reveal healing steps to be taken.

DECLARATION: Flood me, Lord, with all I need to let go and let you handle my battles. Help me to have awareness of the weaknesses of others.

REFLECT ON THE FOLLOWING AND WRITE YOUR THOUGHTS IN YOUR PRAYER JOURNAL:

- YOUR WORDS TO JESUS

- IDEAS AND WORDS FROM JESUS

PRAYER: *Dearest Heavenly Father, I come to seek your Grace in my life to overcome the darkness with Your Light. I need you, Lord. I seek forgiveness, Lord, for any part I have played to bring circumstances to our marriage. I strive to live in your Peace, Lord contending with your contentment. Contentment comes from forgiveness, Lord, so I thank you. Grant me your abiding peace, Lord, to quickly settle any issues with conviction and let go of any bitter root attached to them. Thank you, Jesus, for blessing my marriage. Lord reveal the ways to walk more closely with you, Lord. In Yeshua's Precious and Matchless Name, Amen*

CONCLUSION

ASCRIBE TO THE LORD—For Thine is the Kingdom, the Power and the Glory Forever and Ever. Amen

SERVE OTHERS FOR TRANSFORMATION—
WHEN YOU ARE SERVING OTHERS
YOU ARE SERVING THE LORD WITHIN THEM.

With a deepening Faith, you are called to be an Encourager. You are equipped by the Lord to step into His Holy Spirit Power! You are to be known by His Love through your courage. Seek to understand God's Love through His Living, Breathing Word. He will strengthen you. Seek the Lord with all your heart and soul, and spirit. You are the vessel of the Lord. As the Potter, He created you to believe in Him and carry out His Commands. Love One Another. You belong to Him. He needs you specifically right where you are planted. He needs your prayers right where you are in His Mighty Name. Yes, and Amen. When you demonstrate your deep hunger for God you draw near. He will draw near to you. You will be equipped with His Favor as you become a doer of His Word. Draw a line in the sand to align with His Kingdom, His Power, and His Glory forever and ever. You become His New Wineskin. *You step into a Royal Priesthood of being His Bride.* Soon, and in a while, you will find yourself in *a new place.* Your faith-filled life will blossom. Astonishing Joy takes over, and nothing can stop it. Ascribe to the Lord and step out in faith born out of His Love for you. Exalt the Lord and give Him All Glory for soon and very soon, He is coming. Please read **Romans 10:9-13**.

When, not if, your partner is ready to ask Christ to come into their heart, help them take the vital step with this prayer. It will be the most critical decision of a lifetime. Speak these words: *"Jesus, I repent and confess that I am a sinner. I am so sorry. I ask you to forgive me. I open the door of my heart and invite you to come in and become my Lord and Savior. I believe that you are the Son of God and that you shed your precious blood on the cross for me. Cleanse my heart from all unrighteousness. I give you control over my life, Lord, so that your will can be accomplished in my life. Thank You for saving me now. Amen"*

The moment a heart is given to the Lord, His Spirit enters in to bring guidance and comfort. Holy Spirit will anoint them and teach in the ways of the Lord. He will be with them everywhere they go. They will learn quickly. Jesus is the answer to everything. It is essential to understand the importance of the Anointing of the Holy Spirit Power (**Acts:38-39**) will help them repent and be Born Again from Above. This forgiveness becomes a promise of their inheritance. Your children are included as you daily have a fresh anointing. Immerse yourself in Him as the Holy Spirit will draw the Father near to you. (**James 4:8**) Come near to Jesus to be filled with His Overflowing Astonishing Joy. This is how you will know God, know the truth and be free from sin. Unshakeable peace comes.

Perfect peace comes as you trust Him to bring belief and healing to you and your marriage partner. (**Romans 15:13**) Surrender your life to be filled with His Holy Spirit Power. Surrender your fears, all of them. Holy Spirit will move you from a life of worries to a glorious infilling of

His Hope with expectancy of God's Goodness. You must daily die to yourself. Ask your Holy Spirit to reveal God's Word to guide you. Remember to walk the narrow way by pursuing, practicing, and discerning righteousness. Ascribe in these ways for Jesus, our Living Hope, to bless our unions, families, churches, cities, states, and nations. Yes, and Amen.

"Ascribe to the Lord, you heavenly beings, ascribe to the Lord glory and strength. Ascribe to the Lord the glory due his name; worship the Lord in the splendor of his holiness."

—Psalm 29:1-2 (NIV)

"Yet you, Lord are our Father. We are the clay you are the potter; we are all the work of your hands."

—Isaiah 64:8 (NIV)

"There are the words of him who is holy and true, who holds the key of David. What he opens no one can shut, and what he shuts no one can open. I know your deeds. See, I have placed before you an open door that no one can shut."

—Revelation 3:7 (NIV)

"This is why we must not fall asleep, as the rest do but keep wide awake and clearheaded. But since we belong to the day, we must stay alert and clearheaded by placing the breastplate of faith and love over our hearts, and a helmet of the hope of salvation over our thoughts."

—1 Thessalonians 5:6,8 (TPT)

"I keep asking that the God of our Lord Jesus Christ, the glorious Father, may give you the Spirit of wisdom and revelation, so that you may know him better. I pray that the eyes of your heart may be enlightened in order that you may know the hope to which he has called you, the riches of his glorious inheritance in his holy people, and his incomparably great power for us who believe."

—Ephesians 1:17-19 (NIV)

"…Oh that you would bless me and enlarge my territory! Let your hand be with me and keep me from harm so that I will be free from pain."

—1 Chronicles 4:10 (NIV)

"I am convinced that my God will fully satisfy every need you have, for I have seen the abundant riches of glory revealed to me through Jesus Christ! And God our Father will receive all the glory and the honor throughout the eternity of eternities! Amen."

—Philippians 4:19-20 (TPT)

"Everyone who calls on the name of the Lord will be saved."

—Romans 10:13 (NIV)

"Look, I am coming soon! My reward is with me, and I will give to each person according to what they have done. I am the Alpha and the Omega, the First and the Last, the Beginning and the end."

—Revelations 22:12-13 (NIV)

"Yes, I am coming soon."

—Revelation 22:20 (NIV)

"So, this is my parting command: Love one another deeply!"

—John 15:17 (TPT)

As His Bride, The Lord Jesus Christ calls you to *prepare now* and *make ready* to bring His Purpose and Plan to help expand the Kingdom, which cries out for revival. Look around you and see the chaos. You are called to be bold with your voice, be His Warriors Bride, and take your position as a Kingdom Citizen to give Him all glory through your talents. Are you ready to transform yourself? Ready to become a new wineskin to hold the new creation He is doing through you? (**Isaiah 43:19**) Expect to become like a tree planted by streams of water. (**Psalms 1:3**) Whatever you do will prosper. You didn't choose Jesus; he chose you and anointed you that you would go forth and bear fruit, lasting fruit. Whatever you ask in His Name, the Father will give you. This is His Command: Love each other.

"You did not choose me, but I chose you and appointed you so that you might go and bear fruit—fruit that will last—and so that whatever you ask in my name the Father will give you."

—John 15:16 (NIV)

CHEF NOTE: May you be the one person who has gleaned something from The Astonishing Joy Novella to begin the process of transformation from within and renewal through the Mind of Christ. My time and devotion to the Lord will be a testimony to the Lord through you. It will cause you to flourish in your personal commitments to Him and spill over to your partner, your family, and all who know you. Expect that it will come back with such a rich Triune Blessing for both you and me. I hope to know you as my friend, as my cooking partner, and pray one day we will bake together a cake of Hope and Glory. Together, with Jesus, we will come to the table to have tea, savor the cake, and pray this thing through. Go to the Throne Room of Grace to seek and find the Love Jesus has for you.

"Concerning that day and exact hour no one knows when it will arrive, not the angels of heaven, no even the Son—only the Father knows. This is why you much be waiting, watching ad prayer, because no one knows when that season of time will come."

—Mark 13:32-22 (TPT)

"Now to the One Who is able to keep you without stumbling and to stand before His Glory blameless in extreme joy, to the only God, our Savior through our Lord Yeshua Messiah be glory, majesty, strength and power before every age both now and forever, Amen."

—Jude 1:24-25 (TPT)

PRAYER FOR MY READERS LORD: *Thank you, Lord, to bless anyone reading this book of prayer and devotion. Help them know gratitude uncovers Your Royal Road to Joy. As a Kingdom Ambassador, reveal to them a new calling, Lord, a new purpose for them to do your Will, Father. I delcare and declare the Lord Jesus Christ, the Eternal King of all the earth and the High Priest in the Order of Melchizedek surrounds you with His Healing Love. Align them, Lord, with your impartation of Grace over their marriage unions, Lord. May their marriage be healed with your "Triune God Blessing," which will bless the generations to come. Lord, I ask you to bless their barns, Lord, with a downpouring of prosperity, provision, and your fresh mercy.*

I ask this in the Matchless Name of Yeshua Hamashiach-Messiah / Lord Jesus Christ-Messiah. Amen.

IN REMEMBRANCE

Robert Milton Congdon

May 26, 1936-May 15, 2021

My Precious Beloved Bob gave his Heart to the Lord before Being Called Home. Daily, we spoke the 23rd Psalm to be Restored. May your heart be touched by how the Lord's endless Love brings "Astonishing Joy" and Mercy for His Sons and Daughters. For an account of my tears read "The Called Home Novella," Don't wait to give God all Glory in all you do.

When the Last Hand Comes Aboard

No more a Watch to stand. Old Sailor.
You are outward bound on an ebbing tide.
Eight Bells has rung, and last Watch done.
Now a new Berth waits you on the other side.

Your Ship is anchored in God's Harbor.
And your shipmates, sailors of the Lord,
Are Mustered on deck to greet you,
And pipe you as you come aboard.

Her boilers with full head of steam.
Cargo stowed and Galley stored,
Just waiting to get underway,
When the last Hand comes aboard.

Look sharp! That Hand is you, Old Sailor,
And you'll be sailing out on Heavenly Seas,
May the wind be ever at your back,
Fair weather and God speed!

—Richard John Scarr, England

"Those who sow with tears will reap with Songs of Joy. Those who go out weeping carrying seed to sow, will return with songs of joy, carrying sheaves with them."

—Psalms 126:5-6 (NIV)

TRANSFORMATION:
Mind—Body—Spirit

MIND

"For I know the plans I have for you," declares the Lord, "Plans to prosper you and not to harm you, plans to give you hope and a future."

—Jeremiah 29:11 (NIV)

* * *

Dr. Joseph Peck Webinars to Transform Lives
www.empower2000.com

- IWBNIN Class to reset your mind—Time is Your Life
  I Was Busy Now I'm Not 12 Week Series with Dr. Peck
  www.uncommonjournaling.com/uj-time
- Legacy Dream Team
  www.legacydreamteams.com
- Mentoring with James Goll Series
  www.mentoringwithjames.com
- The Webinar Series from 2019
  Attracting the Favor of God Like a Magnet
  www.attractingfavor.com
- Breaking the Demonic Strongholds Jezebel, Athaliah and
  Delilah
  www.dethroningjezebel2.com—Dr. Sandie Freed

- The Order of Melchizedek
  www.mel777.com—Dr Frances Myles
- Tongues, Power & Blessings
  www.tongues777.com—Apostle Donald Lee
- Forgiveness from the Heart
  www.forgiveness777.com—Craig Hill

Find Your Purpose—Find Yourself

www.on-purpose.com

Prophetic Words including 15 Minutes with Him Blog

www.dutchsheets.org

Prophetic Words—Clay Nash

www.claynash.org

Craig Hill Daily Spirit & Truth

www.craighill.org

Prophetic Words—Chuck Pierce

www.gloryofzion.org

Prophetic Words—Robin Bullock

www.robindbullock.com

Curt Landry Ministries

www.curtlandry.com

Intercessors for America

www.IFApray.org

Kathy Bates: Write-a-Book Roadmap Coach
www.writeabookroadmap.com

Chef Jean Pierre Cooking School
www.chefjeanpierre.com

Piping rock Oils
www.pipingrock.com

BODY

Elevate your Spiritual Life and Body Temple

* * *

Intermittent Fasting Program to Reset the Body
Restore Vitality and Release Unwanted Habits
Restore Beauty with Collagen and Celletoi Skincare Collection
www.YouthfulAgingLifestyle.com

SPIRIT

Achieve Well-Being in your Spirit and Soul

- *Daily Communion with Jesus at your Spiritual Altar*
- *Daily Psalm 91 Prayer of Protection*
- *Daily Psalm 23 Prayer of Protection / Anointing*
- *Daily put on the Armor of God –**Ephesians 6:10***
- *Prayer and Fasting Periods*

* * *

RCP—Rapid Church Planting Ministries
- *Apostle Guenther Hess*
- *Kingdom Building through Training and Prayer Groups*
- *Asia, Europe, Cypress, Africa, and Unreached People Groups*

Dr. Jeff Hazim and Wife Andrea
Shabbat Services Friday Evenings
www.kingdomembassyministeries.org

Pastor Rick Thompson and Wife Debbie
Living Water Community Church
www.lwccftl.org

SMALL GROUP PRAYER TEAMS—FELLOWSHIP

Support Group to Pray, Share and Encourage Each Other
Build Trust, Confidentiality and Accountability
www.ignitejoytoday.com

BOOKS THAT TRANSFORM

Dangerous Prayers, Dr. Francis Myles
Demonic Strongholds Seminar, Dr. Sandie Freed
Family ID, Greg Gunn
Good Morning Holy Spirit, Benny Hinn
Humility and Absolute Surrender, Andrew Murray
Intercession, Reese Howells

In the Wilderness, Loren Helms

I Was Busy Now I'm Not, Dr. Joseph Peck

Prayers that avail much, Germaine Copeland

Restraining Orders, Dr. Francis Myles

Spark Joy, Marie Kondo

The Ancient Paths, Craig Hill

The Greatest Salesman in the World, Og Mandino

The Life-Changing Joy of Tidying Up, Marie Kondo

The One Year Chronological Bible

The Order of Melchizedek, Dr. Francis Myles

The Power of a Parent's Blessing, Craig Hill

The Promises of God, Stephen Burton

The Prophetic Voice of God, Lana Vawser

The Seer, James Goll

The United Methodist Hymnal

Tongues, Donald Lee

Total Forgiveness, R. T. Kendall

Understanding your Dreams, Dr. Sandie Freed

Walking in the Favor of God Video, Dr. Mike Evan

JOY SCRIPTURES (NIV)

FIND YOUR FAVORITE!

1 Chronicles 16:27 *"Splendor and majesty are before him; strength and **joy** are in his dwelling place."*

Psalm 4:7 *"Fill my heart with **joy** when their grain and new wine abound."*

Psalm 5:11 *"But let all who take refuge in you be glad; let them ever sing for **joy**. Spread your protection over them, that those who love your name may rejoice in you."*

Psalm 16:11 *"You make known to me the path of life; you will fill me with **joy** in your presence with eternal pleasure at your right hand."*

Psalm 19:8 *"The precepts of the Lord are right giving **joy** to the heart. The commands of the Lord are radiant giving light to the eyes."*

Psalm 20:4 *"May we shout for **joy** over your victories and lift our banners in the name of our God."*

Psalm 21:1 *"The king rejoices in your strength Lord. How great is his **joy** in the victories you give."*

Psalm 21:6 *"Surely you have granted him unending blessings and made him glad with the **joy** of your presence."*

Psalm 28:7 *"The Lord is my strength and my shield; my heart trust in him and he helps me. My heart leaps for **joy**, and with my song I praise him."*

Psalm 35:9 *"My soul shall be **joyful** in the Lord. And delight in his salvation."*

Psalm 51:12 *"Restore to me the **joy** of your salvation and grant me a willing spirit, to sustain me."*

Psalm 65:13 *"The meadows are covered with flocks and the valleys are mantled with grain; they shot for **joy** and sing."*

Psalm 66:1 *"Shout for **joy** to God all the earth!"*

Psalm 68:3 *"But may the righteous be glad and rejoice before God; may they be happy and **joyful**."*

Psalm 71:23 *"My lips will shout for **joy** when I sing praise to you—I whom you have delivered."*

Psalm 81:1 *"Sing for **joy** to God our strength; shout aloud to the God of Jacob!"*

Psalm 82:4 *"For you make me glad by your deeds Lord; I will sing for **joy** at what your hands have done."*

Psalm 92:4 *"For you make me glad by your deeds Lord; I sing for **joy** at what your hands have done."*

Psalm 100:1 *"Shout for joy to the Lord all the earth."*

Psalm 119:111 *"Your statutes are my heritage forever; they are the joy of my heart."*

Psalm 126:3 *"The Lord has done great things for us, and we are filled with joy."*

Psalm 126:5 *"Those who sow with tears will reap with songs of joy."*

Psalm 132:9 *"May your praise be clothed with your righteousness; may your faithful people sing for joy"*

Psalm 132:16 *"I will clothe her priests with salvation, and her faithful people will ever sing for joy."*

Psalm 149:5 *"Let his faithful people rejoice in this honor and sing for joy on their beds."*

Proverbs 10:28 *"The prospect of the righteous is joy, but the hopes of the wicked come to nothing."*

Isaiah 9:3 *"You have enlarged the nation and increased their joy;"*

Isaiah 12:3 *"With joy you will draw water from the wells of salvation."*

Isaiah 35:10 *"They will enter Zion with singing; everlasting joy will crown their heads."*

Isaiah 51:11 *"Gladness and joy will overtake them, and sorrow and sighing will flee away."*

Isaiah 55:12 *"You will go out in* **joy** *and be led forth in peace;"*

Isaiah 60:5 *"Then you will look and be radiant your heart will throb and swell with* **joy** *the wealth on the seas will be brought to you to you the riches of nations will come."*

Isaiah 61:3 *"Provide for those who grieve in Zion, to bestow on them a crown of beauty instead of ashes; the oil of* **joy** *instead of mourning."*

Isaiah 65:14 *"My servants will sing out of the* **joy** *of their hearts."*

Jeremiah 15:16 *"When you words came, I ate them; they were my* **joy** *and my heart's delight."*

Jeremiah 31:12 *"They will come and shout for* **joy** *on the heights of Zion."*

Jeremiah 33:6 *"Then this city will bring me renown,* **joy***, praise and honor before all nations on earth that hear of all the good things I do for it;"*

Jeremiah 33:11 *"The sounds of* **joy** *and gladness, the voices of bride and bridegroom and the voice of those who bring their offerings to the house of the lord."*

Habakkuk 3:18 *"Yet I will rejoice in the Lord; I will be* **joyful** *in God my Savior."*

Zechariah 10:7 *"Their children will see it and be* **joyful***; their hearts will rejoice in the Lord."*

Matthew 28:8 *"So the women hurried away from the tomb, afraid yet filled with* **joy** *and ran to tell his disciples."*

Luke 2:10 *"But the angel said to them, 'Do not be afraid. I bring you good news that will cause great **joy** for all people.'"*

Luke 6:22 *"Rejoice in that day and leap for **joy** because great is your reward in heaven."*

Luke 15:10 *"In the same way, I tell you there is **joy** in the presence of the angels of God over one sinner who repents."*

Luke 24:52 *"Then they worshiped him and returned to Jerusalem with great **joy**."*

John 15:11 *"I have told you this so that my **joy** may be in you and that your **joy** may be complete."*

John 16:20 *"Very truly I tell you, you will weep and mourn while the world rejoices and will grieve but your grief will turn to **joy**."*

John 16:22 *"So with you; now is your time of grief, but I will see you again and you will rejoice and no one will take away your **joy**."*

John 16:24 *"Until now you have not asked for anything in my name. Ask and you receive, and your **joy** will be complete."*

John 17:13 *"I am coming to you now, but I say these things while I am still in the world, so that they may have the full measure of my **joy** within them."*

Acts 2:28 *"You have made known to me the paths of life; you will fill me with **joy** in your presence."*

Acts 8:8 *"So there was great **joy** in that city."*

Acts 13:52 *"And the disciples were filled with joy and with the Holy Spirit."*

Romans 12:12 *"Be joyful in hope, patient in affliction, faithful in prayer."*

Romans 14:17 *"For the kingdom of God is not a matter of eating and drinking, but of righteousness, peace and joy."*

Romans 15:13 *"May the God of hope fill you with all joy and peace as you trust in him, so that you may overflow with hope by the power of the Holy Spirit."*

2 Corinthians 1:24 *"Not that we lord it over your faith, but we work with you for your joy, because it is my faith you stand firm."*

2 Corinthians 7:4 *"I have spoken to you with great frankness I take great pride in you. I am greatly encouraged; in all our troubles my joy knows no bounds."*

2 Corinthians 8:2 *"In the midst of a very severe trial, their overflowing joy and their extreme poverty welled up in rich generosity."*

Galatians 5:22 *"The fruits of the Spirit are love, joy, peace, forbearance, kindness, goodness, faithfulness, Gentleness, and self-control."*

1 Thessalonians 1:6 *"You became imitators of us and of the Lord, for you welcomed the message in the midst of severe suffering with the joy given by the Holy Spirit."*

Hebrews 10:24 *"You suffered along with those in prison and joyfully accepted the confiscation of your property, because you know that you yourselves had better and lasting possessions."*

Hebrews 12:2 *"Fixing our eyes on Jesus, the pioneer and perfector of faith. For the joy set before him he endured the cross scorning its shame and sat down at the right hand of the throne of God."*

James 1:2 *"Consider it pure joy, my brothers and sisters, whenever you face trials of many kinds."*

1 Peter 1:8 *"Though you have not seen him, you love him and even though you do not see him now you believe in him and are filled with an inexpressible and glorious joy."*

1 John 1:4 *"We write this to make our joy complete."*

Jude 24 *"To him who is able to keep you from stumbling and to present you before his glorious presence without fault and with great joy."*

DI'S NOVELLA RECIPES

MOM'S KEEPER:
RELISHES, JAMS AND PICKLES!

SWEET RELISH

Ingredients:

8 cups green tomatoes

3 T salt

8 cups chopped celery

8 cups ground onions

4 cups ground red peppers

4 cups ground green peppers

1 quart sliced sweet pickles

8 chopped Jonathan Apples

1 ½ quarts vinegar

5 pounds sugar

Cooking Instructions:

Grind tomatoes with salt. Let stand 3 hours. Drain well.

Add celery, onions, red and green peppers, pickles, and apples. Combine all together.

Boil vinegar and sugar until sugar is dissolved.

Add other ingredients.

Stir gently; bring to boil.

Boil 20 minutes.

Pack in sterilized jars and seal at once.

CHOW-CHOW RELISH

Ingredients:

½ peck green tomatoes

6 large onions or 2 cups dried onion flakes

6 green peppers

6 red peppers

4 cups granulated sugar

1 pint vinegar

½ teaspoon turmeric

2 T celery seed

2 T mustard seed

2 T salt

2 whole cloves

Cooking Instructions:

Wash the vegetables.

Grind tomatoes and peppers through coarsest knife on grinder.

Drain well through colander.

Grind onions.

Mix sugar, vinegar, salt, and spices (tied in a bag) and bring to a boil.

Boil 2 minutes, then add ground vegetables.

Heat to boiling. Simmer 3 minutes.

Seal in hot sterilized jars.

RHUBARB JAM

Mom loved Rhubarb!
2 recipes makes 5 pints

Ingredients:

5 cups cut rhubarb

1 small box Strawberry Jello – regular not sugar free

1 cup crushed pineapple with juice

4 cups sugar

Cooking Instructions:

Mix rhubarb pineapple and sugar together and bring to rolling boil.
Add jello and boil for 20 minutes.

Cool. Pour into glasses and refrigerate or seal in regular sealed jars.
Must be refrigerated after opening.

LAZY HOUSEWIFE PICKLES

Dad kept bringing in more cucumbers from his garden!

Ingredients:

20 slices of onions

5 quarts sliced cucumbers

4 cups sugar

½ cup salt

1 pint water

1 quart vinegar

2 ½ teaspoons celery seed

2 ½ teaspoons dill seed

5/8 teaspoon alum

5-quart jars

Cooking Instructions:

Place 4 slices onion in jars, then sliced cucumbers on top.

Combine sugar, salt, water and vinegar. Heat to boiling.

Add to each jar ½ teaspoon each of celery, dill seed and 1/8 teaspoon alum.

Fill jars with boiling syrup and seal.

Refrigerate 2 weeks before using.

CHICKEN FAMILY FAVORITES

TACO-FLAVORED CHICKEN PLATTER

Makes 4-6 Servings

Ingredients:

1 ¼ ounce package taco seasoning mix

½ teaspoon salt

¼ teaspoon garlic powder

3 whole chicken breasts, boned, skinned, cut into quarters

1 (16-ounces) can sliced baby tomatoes

1 (6-ounce) can pitted ripe olives, drained, sliced

¼ cup chopped green onions

1 (4-ounces) can green chilies, drained, chopped

½ cup chicken broth

2 tablespoons cornstarch

1 cup (8-ounces) dairy sour cream

1 cup (4 ounces) crushed tortilla chips

¼ cup shredded Cheddar cheese

Cooking Instructions:

Set Oven 350 degrees

In a pie plate or shallow dish combine taco seasoning, salt and garlic powder.

Coat chicken pieces with taco seasoning mixture and arrange in a 12x8x2-inch dish.

Arrange tomatoes, olives (reserve some for garnish), onions and green chilies over the chicken.

Pour over chicken broth and bake in 350 Oven for 20 minutes.

Top with sour cream, crushed tortilla chips and cheese.

Garnish with remaining olive slices. Taco Lovers Arise!

CHICKEN NICOISE SALAD

Adapted from Cuisine at Home, 2002
Makes 4 servings.

For the Salad:

BOIL:

> 1 ½ lbs small red potatoes
>
> 4 Large Eggs

BLANCH:

> ¼ lb. green beans stemmed
>
> SAUTE in 1t Olive Oil
>
> 2 boneless, skinless chicken breast halves, seasoned with salt and pepper

PREPARE:

> 1-pint grape tomatoes, halved
>
> ½ cup niçoise or kalamata olives, pitted and halve

For the Vinaigrette:

WHISK TOGETHER:

    ¼ cup fresh lemon juice

    2 T minced fresh tarragon

    1 T shallot, minced

    1 T Dijon mustard

    2 t. anchovy paste (necessary yet won't taste!)

    1 t. honey

    2/3 cup extra-virgin olive oil

    Salt and pepper to taste

I like adding:

    Chopped Red Onion—chopped ½ red onion

    Sliced Cucumber—thin slice cucumber

    Capers as desired

BOIL potatoes until done and hard-cooked eggs.

    Slice potatoes ¼ inch thick.

    Add vinaigrette to warm potatoes to enhance flavor.

    Blanche green beans 5 minutes and add to potato mixture.

    Chop eggs for garnish and set aside.

SAUTE chicken in oil over medium-high heat until cooked through (about 8 minutes per side).

    Cut into ¼ thick slices.

PREPARE tomatoes and olives

Add to mixture and optional onion, cucumber, and capers.

TOSS lightly to coat all the items and transfer to a platter.

Add egg garnish! Awesome supper dish!!!

CYNCY'S CURRIED CHICKEN SALAD

My Sister-in-law is one great cook!
Makes 4-6 Servings

For the Salad:

3 cups cooked, diced Chicken (4 chicken breast halves) Bake in ½ cup half/half, seasoned about 17-20 minutes

½-¾ t salt

¼ t pepper

1 T curry

1 cup finely diced celery

¼ cup sliced scallions

Sauce:

1 cup mayo

½ cup Major Grey's Chutney

1 cup chopped honey roasted almonds

1 cup seedless grapes halved

Optional:

    1 T lemon juice

    ¼ cup raisins

    ½ cup red onion chopped

Cooking Instructions:

Prepare chicken, celery, grapes, almonds and scallions and optional items.

Prepare sauce, combine, and enjoy!!

Cyncy says Bon Appetit!

HEAVENLY ANGEL FOODS

MOM'S ANGEL FOOD CAKE

I remember the 12 egg whites.

Ingredients:

1 ½ cups sugar

1 cup flour

½ teaspoon salt

12 egg whites, room temperature

1 ½ teaspoon cream of tartar

1 teaspoon vanilla extract

½ teaspoon almond extract (my optional addition)

Cooking Instructions:

Preheat oven to 325F

Sift ½ cup sugar, the flour, and salt together several times

Beat the egg whites in a large mixer bowl until foamy.

Sprinkle with the cream of tartar and beat until stiff but not dry.

Beat in the vanilla and almond extract. Then beat in the remaining 1 cup of sugar—2 tablespoons at a time. Beat until the peaks are stiff and glossy.

Gently fold 1/3 flour mixture at a time into the egg white mixture.

Pour the batter into an ungreased 10-inch tube pan.

Bake on lowest rack.

Bake until the cake springs back when lightly touched 1 hour.

Invert the pan over the neck of a wine bottle.

Let it cool for several hours.

Run a knife around the side of the pan to loosen the cake and invert on to a platter.

Serve with toppings.

Topping:

Serve with sweetened whipped cream and fresh berries.

Serve with Chocolate Sauce

    4 ounces semisweet chocolate, broken into small pieces

    ¼ cup unsweetened cocoa powder

    ½ cup water

    Heat the chocolate, cocoa and water in a heavy small saucepan over medium-low heat, stirring constantly, until smooth. Serve warm

    Make 1 cup

Surely the angels make their cake and ate it too!
My mother is my angel.

GERMAN CHOCOLATE BARS OR 2 LAYER CAKE

(**Chef Note:** The *Angel Food Cake takes 12 Egg whites while the German Chocolate Bars with Coconut Frosting uses 12 egg yokes!*

It makes for a dynamic duo! Bars freeze well!)

Ingredients:

2 ¼ cups whole wheat four

1/3 cup powdered milk

½ cup water, boiling

2 cups sugar

1 cup butter

¼ cup cornstarch

1 teaspoon baking soda

4-oz package German Sweet Chocolate

9 egg yolks

1 tablespoon vinegar

½ cup water

Cooking Instructions:

Sift whole wheat flour cornstarch, powdered milk and soda.

Break German Chocolate Bar into boiling water to soften.

Combine sugar, egg yolks and butter.

Add the vinegar, remaining water and chocolate.

Stir in the flour mixture and blend well.

Bake in lightly greased 12 17-inch baking pan for 40 minutes at 350F.

This recipe may also be made into a layer cake by baking two 9-inch round cake pans

Frost bars or cake with Coconut Frosting.

Coconut Frosting:

Ingredients:

1 cup sugar

¾ cup evaporated milk

1 7-oz package coconut

3 egg yolks

¼ cup butter

½ cup nuts chopped

Cooking Instructions:

Blend sugar, egg yolks and milk in small pan.

Add butter.

Bring to a boil, stirring constantly.

Add coconut and nuts.

Frost bars.

DI'S FAMOUS CHOCOLATE CAKE

From the Cookies, Cookies and More Bakery, St. Louis, Mo, 1980s

Chocolate Brownie Cake Ingredients:

1 ¼ sticks sweet butter

4 ounces unsweetened chocolate

4 eggs

2 cups sugar (I use turbinado sugar – partially refined sugar which retains molassas)

1 teaspoon vanilla

1 cup flour

2 cups pecans chopped

Cooking Instructions:

Melt chocolate and butter, then cool.

Mix well with eggs, sugar, and vanilla.

Mix four and pecans together and add to the above.

Bake in two 8-inch greased and lined cake pans at 310F degrees for 30 minutes. Do NOT overbake. Check center to make sure toothpick comes clean but not dry.

****BIG SECRET NOW: for best results put a pan of water in oven underneath pans while baking. Cake will be moist. Cool. Ice first layer then finish both layers.

Icing Ingredients:

1 stick butter

5 cups of powdered sugar (a box has only 4 cups)

1 cup heavy cream

1 teaspoon vanilla

1 cup cocoa

2 ounces unsweetened chocolate melted and cooled.

Cooking Instructions:

Cream butter.

Add powdered sugar, cream with butter.

Add cream, vanilla, cocoa, and melted chocolate.

Mix well. Ice cake.

Optional:

Sprinkle ½ cup chopped pecans on top.

Nice to serve with whipped cream or ice cream.

Offer this as a gift to make a heart sing!

14 CARAT CAKE

Cyncy's Awesome Carrot Cake
(Will keep 2-3 weeks in refrigerator if covered)

Ingredients:

2 cups sifted flour

2 tsp. baking powder

1 ½ tsp baking soda

1 ½ tsp salt

2 tsp cinnamon

2 cups sugar

1 ½ cups salad oil

4 eggs

2 cups finely grated carrots

1 8 ½ oz can crushed pineapple well-drained

½ cup chopped nuts

Cooking Instructions:

Sift together flour, baking powder, baking soda, salt, and cinnamon.

Add sugar, salad oil and eggs. Mix well.

Add carrots, pineapple, and nuts. Blend thoroughly.

Pour into three 9" round cake pans that have been greased and floured.

Bake in moderate oven (350) 35-40 minutes. Test with a toothpick.

Cool ten minutes in pans. Turn out on wire racks and cool thoroughly.

Fill layers and frost top and sides of cake with cream cheese frosting.

CREAM CHEESE FROSTING

Ingredients:

½ cup butter

1 8 oz package cream cheese

1 tsp vanilla

1 lb. confectioner's sugar, sifted

Cooking Instructions:

Combine butter, cream cheese and vanilla. Cream well.

Add confectioners' sugar gradually, beating well. If mixture too thick to spread, add a small amount of milk.

Can put chopped nuts around sides of cake

To serve 250 multiply by 12!!!

MOM'S HOMEMADE APPLE CRUMBLE

Apple Crumble was Mom's Go To Dessert! We loved Mom's pies! Homemade Apple Pie Sweetness!

Serves 10

Ingredients:

2 ½ cups old-fashioned oats

1 ½ cups (packed) golden brown sugar

1 cup all-purpose flour

1 cup (2 sticks) chilled unsalted butter, cut into ½ inch cubes

Nonstick vegetable oil spray

4 pounds large Granny Smith:

    Apples, peeled, halved, cored

    Each half cut into 6 slices

3 T fresh lemon juice

1 T ground cinnamon

Vanilla Ice Cream

Cooking Instructions:

Mix oats, 1 cup sugar and flour in bowl.

Add butter; rub in with fingertips until topping comes together in moist clumps (Can be made a day ahead)

Preheat oven to 375 Degrees.

Spray 13x9x2-inch glass baking dish with Non-stick spray.

Mix apples, lemon juice, cinnamon, and ½ cup brown sugar in bowl.

Transfer to dish. Spring topping over.

Bake crumble until apples are tender and topping is brown and crisp, about 55 minutes. Cool slightly.

Spoon warm crumble into bowls.

Serve with Ice Cream. You will love it!

ESCAPADE GALLEY HOLIDAY MEALS

WILDRICE CHICKEN CASSEROLE

Family Favorite—Great for Entertaining
8 Servings

Ingredients:

1 cup wild rice—cooked in 2 cups salted water

½ cup chopped onion

½ cup butter 1 stick

¼ cup whole wheat flour

1 ½ cup fresh mushroom sliced and sauteed in butter

1 ½ cup chicken broth

½ cup heavy cream (I use some of remainder on top before baking)

2 chicken whole chicken breasts (cooked in cream or milk seasoned salt 17 minutes or so)

¼ cup diced pimento

2 tablespoons parsley chopped

1 ½ teaspoon salt

1 ½ teaspoon pepper (be careful not to overdo this)

½ cup sliced almonds (prefer sliced to slivered)

Cooking Instructions:

350F oven in greased 2-quart casserole dish. 30 minutes.

Wash rice well and cook in 2 cups of water + salt (1/2t) about an hour until tender.

In deep saucepan cook onion in butter until clear.

Add flour and stir well.

Cook until mixed in.

Gradually add chicken broth to thicken the mixture.

Add cream to create a white sauce.

After thickened add rice, mushroom, diced chicken, pimento, parsley, salt and pepper.

Mix well.

Add to greased casserole dish and top with sliced almonds.

Bake 350F 30 minutes or until Bubbling well on the edges.

Additional Notes:

Can be prepared ahead same day to refrigerator. Take out 1 ½ hours

Ahead of baking to bring back to room temperature.

Freeze leftovers for future quick dinners.

This is our holiday go-to meal! The family loves it!

CHANTERELLE, PORT & VEAL STEW

Chef Jean Pierre's Shiitake, Port and Beef Stew—Di's Variation
Makes 8 Servings

Ingredients:

1 cup White Port Wine

1 cup dried Chanterelle Mushrooms

1 T extra virgin olive oil

4 pounds of veal breast pieces

20 pearl onions (fresh 1 Bag)

1 T fresh garlic, minced

1 cup chopped onion

20 baby carrots (1-1/2 inches long)

2 cans diced tomatoes drained

¼ cup tomato puree

3 T fresh thyme

2 T fresh sage

1 T fresh rosemary

1 bay leaf

5 cups chicken stock (Imagine)

¼ salt

½ pepper

2 packages of dried sweet cherries or 1 can dark cherries pitted

1 T cornstarch dissolved in 2T water (optional)

1 T chopped parsley

Cooking Instructions:

In a saucepan, heat the Port, when hot add the Chanterelles and let cook at a

very low heat for 10 minutes.

Divide the veal into 2 batches. Pat dry, layout small veal pieces and season each batch with 1 T of fresh thyme, 1 T sage, salt and pepper on both sides.

Brown well in skillet on both sides.

Repeat with second batch.

In Dutch oven, heat olive oil, add chopped onion and sweat. Salt lightly.

Add garlic

WHEN FRAGRANT add veal with their juices, carrots, pearl onions, tomatoes, tomato puree, last 1 T thyme, rosemary, bay leaf, chicken stock and port wine with chanterelles.

Reduce heat to low, let simmer 1 ½-2 hours, stirring occasionally, until the veal is very tender.

Add the dried cherries, adjust the seasoning with salt and pepper and simmer for 15 more minutes. Adjust the thickness with corn starch if necessary to bubbling sauce.

Sprinkle with freshly chopped parsley!!

LOVELY WITH GARLIC YUKON GOLD MASHED POTATOES

This is such a great winter comfort dish—great for entertainment!

MOM'S BAKED OYSTER CASSEROLE

This is a family favorite especially at Christmas.

Ingredients:

3 cups soda crackers crumbs

4 eggs hard boiled, shells removed

2 cans 8-oz cans oysters, drained, save liquid

2-3 cups of milk

3 tablespoons butter

Cooking Instructions:

Set oven 350F.

Crush crackers to fine pieces and place in greased baking dish.

Cut eggs into pieces slices and place over the crushed crackers

Drain oysters (if large cut into pieces) and layer over eggs.

Heat oyster liquid and pour over all the ingredients.

Put pats of butter over on top of the layers.

Heat the milk to boiling point and mix into dish stirring until blended.

Bake until hot and browned. About 45 minutes.

DAD'S FAVORITE KOLACHES RECIPE

Mom developed great skills in cooking Dad's favorite Czechoslovakian foods!' My brother and I grew up on these Czech delights!

Ingredients:

1 ½ cup scalded milk

2/3 cup sugar

2/3 cup shortening (lard)

2 eggs

1-package yeast or yeast cake

½ cup mashed potatoes

2 teaspoons salt

6 ½ cups sifted flour

Cooking Instructions:

Scald Milk and add shortening salt sugar and mashed potatoes. Cool

Add yeast and about 2 cups flour. Beat well then ass rest of flour and knead down and let rise again.

Form small balls and arrange them on greased cookie sheets.

When light to touch make an impression in the center of each with your fingertips. Then, fill with ay kind of filling.

Let rise again for about 15 minutes or until lite to touch.

Bake at 425F for 10-12 minutes

POPPYSEED FILLING

Ingredients:

2 cups poppy seeds

2 cups cream

2 cups sugar

4 stiffly beaten eggs

Cooking Instructions:

Grind 2 cups of poppy seeds.

Combine with other ingredients.

Simmer until moisture is absorbed.

Stirring constantly. Cool.

LEMON DAYS OF TROUBLE...MAKE
LEMON BARS

LEMON BARS

What's not to love about a lemon bar!!!
Makes 3 dozen

Ingredients:

CRUST

2 cups unbleached all-purpose flour

½ cup confectioners' sugar

2 sticks butter

FILLING

4 eggs, beaten

6 tablespoons fresh lemon juice (about 4 lemons)

1 teaspoon grated lemon zest

2 cups granulated sugar

1 tablespoon unbleached all-purpose flour

Confectioners' sugar (optional)

Cooking Instructions:

CRUST:

Combine flour and confectioners' sugar in bowl.

Cut in butter with pastry blender or two knives until mixture has a crumbly consistency.

Press into 9x13-inch pan and bake in preheated 350F oven for 20 minutes.

FILLING:

Combine eggs, lemon juice and zest, sugar, flour, and baking powder, beating until smooth.

Pour over baked crust, return to oven, and bake 20-25 minutes.

Remove from the oven and let cool.

Sprinkle with additional confectioners' sugar, if desired.

What a great way to recover from a troubling day!!!!

BIBLIOGRAPHY

I am grateful to give credit to the many prophetic and spiritually gifted ones who have offered classes and written books that I have read or under whom I have studied to honor them as mentors on my Spiritual Journey. They include:

Bullock, Robin, "Episode 21," Robin Bullock Ministries, interview by Steve Schultz, *Elijah Streaming* with Steve Schultz, September27,2021/ https://youtu.be/_o2JRyAZ98g Chapter 1.

Evans, Dr. Mike, "Walking in the Favor of God", Jerusalem Prayer Team, Video Presentation,December 18, 2018 https://youtu.be/ wLfvUw6n3BM Chapter 1.

Freed, Sandie. *Dethroning Jezebel (Part 2)-Breaking the Demonic Threefold cord of Jezebel, Athaliah, and Delilah.* Lesson 6 Establishing a Victory Structure Study Guide, presented by Empower 2000 Kingdom Based Webinars, August 2020. Chapter 2.

Goll, James. *Mentoring with James Goll Series.* Presented by Empower 2000 Kingdom Based Webinars, Fall 2017. Introduction.

Gunn, Greg. Family ID—Intentional Direction: Discover your Family's Unique Purpose and Passion. 2012, Chapter 5.

Helms, Loren W. *A Voice in the Wilderness*. Indiana: Evangel Voice Publications, 1973. with permission from Chapter 27 The Beginning, pages 352 and 352. Chapter 2

Hess, Apostle Guenther, Founder of RCP—*Rapid Church Planting for Home Churches*. Commissioned by God to bring revival to the African nations through Home Churches and the Timothy Bible School Teaching. Also presented in Germany, Finland, Wales, Middle East and Asia. Chapter 2. RCP Intercessor Prayer Team: Paster Stephen Guarneros, Rolland Abraham, Iris Schuman, Carrie Ross, Dianne Congdon, Wendy Holloun, Leah Dent, Joyce Long, Klaas Bakker and Richard Smith.

Hinn, Benny. *Good Morning Holy Spirit*. Tennessee: Thomas Nelson Publishing, 2004. Chapter 1

Hazim, Dr. Jeff. *Cataclysmic Intervention/Genesis 6-11*. Florida: Kingdom Embassy Ministries, October 8, 2021/https://kingdomembassy ministries.org/sermon-notes/ Chapter 1.

Hill, Craig. Family Foundations. Daily Spirit and Truth, "Are you an ambassador of the Kingdom?" February, 2021; The Power of a Parent's Blessing. Florida: Charisma House Book Group, 2013. Chapter 5,7.

Intrater, Asher. *Authority: Biblical Principles of Spiritual and Delegated Authority*. Maryland: Revive Israel Media, 2014. Chapter 3.

Kendall, RT, *Total Forgiveness*. Florida: Chrisma House, 2007. Chapter 5.

Kondo, Marie. *Spark Joy, an illustrated master class on the art of organizing and tidying up. Life-Changing Magic of Tidying Up,* the Japanese art of decluttering and organizing. Great Britain: Ten Speed Press/ am imprint of the Crown Publishing Group, a division of Random House LLC, English Translation by Cathy Hirano, 2016/ 2014, Chapter 6.

Lee, Apostle Donald. *Tongues, Power & Blessings.* Lecture Series presented by Empower 2000 Kingdom Based Webinars, entitled "Warfare that Works," 2021, Chapter 2.

Murray, Andrew. *Humility & Absolute Surrender.* South Carolina: CreateSpace, 2013/2021. Chapter 1,3.

Myles, Dr Francis. *The Order of Melchizedek.* Arizona: Francis Myles International, 2010, Chapter 1, 2, 4.

Peck, Dr. Joseph. *I Was Busy, Now I'm No---Changing the Way You Think About Time.* New York: Morgan James Publishing, 2015, Introduction, Chapter 1,2,3,4.

Prince, Derek. *Orphans Widows, the Poor and Oppressed: God's Heart for the needy.* Edited from a transcript of a message given in November 1999 to the Kensington Temple, London, England. North Carolina: Derek Prince Ministries, 1999. Chapter 6.

United Methodist Worship. *The United Methodist Hymnal,* Tennessee: United Methodist Publishing House, Page 382 "Have Thine Own Way Lord," Words by Adelaide A Pollard, 1902 (Jerimiah 18:6), Music my George C. Stebbins, 1907. "Amazing Grace," Words by John Newton, 1779, based on 1 Chronicles 17:16-17, transcription by Albert Tosi, Music by Edwin O Ecell, 1903. Page 378. "Trust and Obey," Words by John H Sammis 1887 based on 1 John 1:7, Music by Daniel B. Towner, 1887, Page 467. "Great is Thy Faithfulness," Words by Thomas O.

Chisholm, 1923 based on Lamentations 3:22-23, Music William M. Runyan 1923, Page 140. Chapter 2.

Vickler, Mark. *Four Keys to "Hearing God's Voice" Lecture Series—Introduction.* Florida: Communion with God Ministries, October 2019, Chapter 1.

Wilkin Jen, *Women of the Word.* Illinois: Crossway Publishing, 2014, with permission, Chapter 1.

DI'S RECIPES

Cuisine at Home. *Chicken Salad Nicoise,* Iowa: Home Publishing Company, page 15, 2002, adapted.

Cyncy's Chicken Salad, 14 Carrot Cake, Cyncy Abel, Bluffton, North Carolina

Chocolate Brownie Cake, Cookies, Cookies and More Bakery, 1980s

ABOUT
DIANNE CONGDON

Growing up in the 40s and 50s in the small Kansas farming town of Holyrood gave Dianne a foundation of trust and Christian "Love Your Neighbor" values. The quiet kindness of her parents, Frank, and Agnes Jurenka, led her to serve others at a young age. Dianne is a lover of Yeshua/Jesus. He came to her first through the rose wallpaper of her room when she was a little girl. Eye-level, this single rose became the flower that blossomed her into joyous expression. Today, she *exists to serve by igniting joy* in others.

Born Again at age 75, Dianne, now 79, shows us it is never too late to come to the Lord. You will adore her passion for cooking with Chef Notes that will delight every cook! She shares her steps and serves up her joy to help you shift and sift into embracing Jesus in a fresh new way. She will open the door for the Holy Spirit to come in! Dianne lives in Ft. Lauderdale, Florida. Her husband, Bob, was Called Home on May 15th, 2021. They have, between them, 3 children. The Called Home Novella reveals her days of tears which will warm your heart.

Please consider giving Dianne a Review of her book on Amazon and Follow Her there to learn about her next novella! Review her on Good Reads found at www.GoodReads.com.

Dianne would love to meet you. She offers webinars and prayer support groups led by the Holy Spirit. Go to

www.ignitejoytoday.com

DIANNE CAN BE REACHED BY:

Facebook: www.facebook.com/youthfulaginglifestyle
LinkedIn: log onto www.linkedin.com then search for Dianne Congdon, Kingdom Ambassador, Ft. Lauderdale, FL
Website: www.ignitejoytoday.com

Webinars and Zoom Meetings
Zoom with Dianne: (also a great gift idea)
- Schedule meeting with Dianne on her website
- Schedule a Speaking Engagement with Dianne

Gifts:
- The Called Home Novella
- IgniteJoyToday Aprons
- Collagen
- Celletoi Skincare Collection
- Intermittent Fasting

CAROL CARTER

www.carol-carter.com

Carol Carter is an internationally renowned American Artist whose work has been exhibited in six countries and published worldwide. She has won numerous international prizes for her work.

Carol received her MFA from Washington University, St. Louis.

Awarded a MAA-NEA Fellowship in Painting and Works on Paper in 1994, she was voted Best St. Louis Artist by The Riverfront Times In 2000.

Carol has been published in many magazines and books internationally. She has taught in France Norway, Ecuador, Hong Kong, and the US Virgin Islands. She teaches watercolor from coast to coast in the United States.

Among her many accolades, Carol received the Woman in Arts Recognition Award from the National Society of Daughters of American Revolution 2021.

Her work is represented in many public and private art collections.

"The LORD bless you and keep you;
The LORD make His face shine upon you,
And be gracious to you;
The LORD lift up His countenance upon you,
And give you peace."

—Numbers 6:24-26

ABIDING in JOY,

Dianne